Venice in a Day

By Stephen J Bishop

The only guide that shows you how it is and will let
you experience what Venice is really like.

Campo dei Frari

First published in the UK in 2018 by the Cloister House Press.

Email: stephen.bishop4@btopenworld.com

Acknowledgements

The author wishes to thank the following for their kind permission to reproduce their photographs and sections of maps.

>   Photographs: Stephen Bishop, Laurence Bishop, Carol Reed-Bishop and Susan Hadingham.

>   Maps: Storti Edizioni s.r.l, Venice, Italy, pages, 8, 45, 55, 59, 64, 65, 79, 91, 105, 116

Cover photographs:

>   Front - Gondola ride of a lifetime - Gliding gently down the Grand Canal.

>   Back - Serenading on the Grand Canal.

Disclaimer: The information contained in this book is given in good faith and is believed to be correct at the time of publication. No responsibility is accepted by either the author or the publisher for errors or omissions, or for any loss or injury howsoever caused.

Purchase of Further Copies: Further copies of this book may be purchased through book sellers, Amazon or by contacting the author on stephen.bishop4@btopenworld.com stating your requirements. Payment can be made by bank transfer, cheque or PayPal.

Preface - Why this book?

The author of this book is an experienced independent traveller, having been to nearly fifty countries, some of them many times. After having read hundreds of travel guides to research various trips, I am left with the observation and frustration that very few guides give a real picture or a feel of the place you are going to visit. What will it be like when I get there? What are the key things I need to know to `make my life much easier? Many guides are full of hundreds of pages of plain tight text with masses of information or

People enjoying life – Cannaregio

repeated material which you have sort through just to get the few key things you want. Many are not even up to date or are just not telling you what you really need to know in an easily consumable format which you can digest quickly to find what you want. Others are 90% history. If I want a history lesson, I will go and buy a definitive history book or ask Henry VIII or William the Conqueror.

In my view, the main reason for most people wanting to travel is to see the sights and experience the things of interest, and be able to do this easily without the need of a personal tour guide, starting as a minimum in having a clear map as to where all the interesting places are. Most guides are devoid of good maps although they are getting better. I also get the feeling that some of the authors of guides have never really experienced the places they write about at all, damning as that may be - but I am sure in many cases it is true. But some guides do have a place with more detailed information, which can supplement this guide if you want that too. I find that *Time Out, Lonely Planet* and *DK Eyewitness* guides are the better ones.

An experience to enjoy

So what I have set out to achieve in this book, to make it better for the everyday traveller, is to give a pictorial view of what you are going to see, so you can visualise the place and get a feel of it before you go. It is only through genuinely experiencing a place and its people yourself that you can articulate that vision to others.

Cafés and restaurants – San Polo

The other key ingredient I feel is missing from many travel guides is opinions. That is why so many of them come over as grey and boring. It may be by intention that all they want to provide is information. Whether you agree or disagree, differing opinions bring a place and its people to life, and only then can we start the debate of what is good, bad and plain diabolical. I have tried to take opinions from across the demographic age groups, from those who can just about talk and be pushed round the neighbourhood in their buggies, through the more able millennials glued to their mobile phones, to experienced wise old folks who still have that youthful urge to travel and now have a new found freedom in their self-propelled electric buggies, dodging in and out, terrorising the other pedestrians. So there should be something here for everyone.

So, with this book I have tried to set out and achieve the principles above, by illustrating what you will see through pictures, maps and descriptions of how to get around and describing what you will

Glorious seafood in the Rialto Markets

Fontamente Nove – Castello

Canals going everywhere – Castello

find along the way. There are some suggested walks that will get you out on your feet, taking you around the city on an efficient itinerary, seeing the best Venice has to offer, but hopefully without wearing you out in the process.

This guide will give you most of the information you need to be able to get around and explore the Venice in a few days and ensure you do get a worthwhile experience from your visit and want to come back again.

The author has travelled to Venice a number of times over the years, come rain or shine, and walked the alleys and can now do it without a map. Every trip is different, new places to find, new places to eat in and new people to meet. It might not tell you everything, but that is not the purpose. You will see the best, and in any case, it is a good pictorial view of the city which will show you what you should be dreaming about.

And finally, I do hope you will find this guide useful and gives you some inspiration, that it brings Venice to life for you, and that you have a really good experience on your visit. You should do - you never know what you might find out round the next corner. Just keep an open mind and chill.

Wishing you happy exploring and an enjoyable visit.

Stephen Bishop

The mighty Campanile of St Mark's

Traditional hotels in the Dorsodoro

Contents

Striking colours in the backwaters

Chapter 1 – Why We All Fall in Love with Venice

Most of us have dreams of where we would like to go, what we want to do, or where we would like to be at some point in our lives. Some of us have a 'bucket list'; many of us even dream of going to Venice, some of us for many years or decades. We are all different in how we imagine Venice might look when we visit it for the first time. Maybe our dream is to go and see many of the great cities of Europe, study the old masters, cruise around the canals

Gondolas waiting for wealthy customers at the Rialto Bridge

on a luxury boat, live the high life of make believe staying in the Gritti Palace, or just sit outside a bar in the sunshine, hanging out in the city that floats, watching the world go by.

A place for romance

Venice has all of this in abundance, a place of inspiration and many possibilities. We can see it, do it, feel it, and sometimes even smell it, but only very occasionally, it is not as bad as some as some people make out when you get there. It's all about our preconceptions. From my experience as a seasoned traveller, most places are normally much better than you envisage beforehand. It will be different from what you expect. Don't let your preconceptions or negative opinions of others hold you back. Be positive, always make the most of where you are.

Dreams inspire us and drive our sense of purpose, real or unreal. Something very different from our daily lives. Something with that 'wow' factor. Venice can do that too. All we need is an opportunity and the will to do it.

Venice is not just for romantic couples gliding around in each other's aura in gondolas. It is for single travellers too, a very vibrant city, full of beautiful timeless treasures, stunning architecture, the home of grand masters gone by, amazing cathedrals, stunningly beautiful churches, world famous vistas, and more. It is not just a place to see, but to experience too, with over 1500 years of history, timeless treasures, offering lots of time to chill out in those canal-side coffee shops to take it all in.

Artists on street corners

Venice is made up of 118 islands all joined together by 416 bridges. It has 177 canals, 450 palaces and 127 squares or piazzas. The first casino in the world was opened in Venice in 1638, so roll on Las Vegas, it has a long way to go if it ever survives that long before the drinking water runs out. Also in past times, when the human race was a less healthy species, when the plague struck, it was the first city to invent the concept of quarantine.

Separate mazes of alleyways and canals crossing each other's paths every so often

It is a very special place, unique in so many ways and sometimes quirky. Did you know there is a law that it is verboten to feed the pigeons? Anyone who feeds them, does so at their peril, and will incur the wrath of the pigeon police, who will fine you or maybe lock you up in the Doge's Palace, a terrible medieval establishment full of nasties.

Engage with the local people, along Giudecca

Venice is not just seeing someone's 'look at me' posts on Facebook or a travel show on TV; it is experiencing it, being part of it. Like Alice through the Looking Glass when she climbed through the mirror. After traversing the causeway, most people land in Venice in either Piazzale Roma, or the adjacent railway station. It is like going through a door into another world. The real world is on one side and Venice is on the other.

When you enter Venice, you can feel the past, the centre of an ancient empire, the wars, the merchants trading at the hub of numerous trading routes and all the immense wealth from a bygone age. The water and canals are at the heart of the city. There are no cars, just narrow alleys and piazzas, littered with shops, cafés and bars, just like old cities used to be. Seafood is a speciality, with the aquaculture of the lagoon providing very special culinary delights, and very tasty they are too. Many famous artists, writers and musicians were born here, like Canaletto, Giacomo Casanova and Antonio Vivaldi, not to mention the famous Doges. There are carnivals, regattas and regular festivals to add to the mix.

Quiet places to ponder

It is not a place to be rushed on a schedule. It is to be savoured, taking your time to follow your curiosity and letting it take you wherever it will, wandering through the alleyways and getting lost, immersing yourself in the beauty of days gone by. Become part of it and open up your imagination, just like Alice.

Venice is a UNESCO World Heritage site, if that is not a good reason in itself to see it for yourself. It is sinking between 1mm and 2mm a year, another good reason to see it before it disappears with King Canute and the rising tide. It is two cities in one. One on the water, a grid of canals shared by ferries, gondolas and work boats, overlaid by a maze of alleyways and bridges which creates a separate map in itself, with both intersecting at many points and providing stunning views.

The Salute from the Accademia Bridge

Most visitors impatiently head off down the main drag from Piazzale Roma or the railway station, past the Rialto Bridge to St Mark's Square. They then queue for hours to get into the Basilica and the Doge's Palace, sharing the frustrating experience with thousands of others who arrive at the same time, before coming back the same way, or trying to get on the No.1 Vaporetto at prime time, finishing the day exhausted and disappointed. Venice is not just all about St Mark's Square and gondolas - there are many other interesting places and piazzas off the beaten track where you do not have to share your space with hordes of other tourists on a mission. There is the San Nicolo dei Mendicoli church, one of the most spectacular in Venice (check opening times); each time I have visited it, there has been no one else there, even in August. Take a stroll along Giudecca, or a wander round the Ghetto. Here you will see real people, not just tourists and have space.

Queues and crowds at the Basilica – How to avoid them

Venice is a city to see day and night. Although the dark alleys can be a bit intimidating and it is even easier to get lost at night, it is a safe city. There are no drunks, nasty goblins or ghoulie creatures hiding in the gloom. But it is a magic moment when you see the full moon reflecting off the lagoon or take a late night romantic trip up the Grand Canal. Venice comes to life at night. Seemingly derelict restaurants and bars light up and become alive, full of ambiance and atmosphere. Alternatively, be an early bird and go for a wander and enjoy the peace and quiet before the tourists arrive. Piazza San Marco can be a real treat at 5 o'clock in the morning is an inspiring place.

3

Venice is beautiful at night too – San Marco

Behind the crumbling plaster is a maze of winding alleyways, giving Venice a unique character and a charm of its own. Some of the buildings might look ready for demolition, but the elegance of the whole, a city of amazing exception and beauty, is preserved for us to see today. It feels like you have been transported back in time in a Tardis, and are walking through a bygone age, or one of those world-famous canvases where the great painters of previous centuries have trodden the same path before you, where little has changed. You can put yourself in their shoes and see the world the same way they did.

Venice's cuisine will please all Italian loving gourmands with its fresh simplicity and focus on seasonal and local ingredients. The lagoon surrounding the city abounds with delicious fish and seafood, while the Veneto, the greater region where Venice is located, is one of Italy's most fertile and delivers a bounty of fresh fruits and vegetables all year round.

Grand Canal as seen by the old masters at the Rialto

All sorts of wonderful things

So why do we all fall in love with Venice? It's all about how you feel and live your dream to unlock it. It is one of the best places to go to do that. If you are a romantic, with the person of your dreams it can help loosen those inner feelings to share a wonderful experience together. Lose each other in another world the other side of the mirror. But remember Alice was single too and she met all sorts of interesting characters. Engage with the people you meet and take in the ambiance of the environment you are in and chill out.

4

Participate and become part of your dreams. Get blown away and marvel at the beauty of the city. Whatever your preconceptions were before you came, Venice will change them for good and you will come back with a cool set of memories that you will cherish for the rest of your life; that's a promise. You have lived your dream and Venice will make its mark. We can help you do that and show how to make it happen. Let's do it.

And just one more important fact:

"Is it worthwhile to observe that there are no Venetian blinds in Venice?" William Dean Howells.

The leaning church tower of Santo Stefano – San Marco, from the campanile at San Giorgio Maggiore

Smart boats – local water taxi

Canal side eating – alfresco

The Rialto Bridge under a setting sun

Early morning, local shops opening up – Canale di Cannaregio

Chapter 2 – Top 11 Sights at a Glance

It is hard to determine what are the best top 10 sights in Venice because there are so many to see, either in terms of importance or variety, so I have made it 11 because I couldn't make it less. The final list has been selected to try and suit everyone, selections based on their uniqueness, because there's nothing like it anywhere else in the world, or it's an experience you can become involved in that you will never forget, or it just simply blows your mind away. Some may charge, but others are also free.

Fondazione Bevilacqua La Masa

It can be worse than this, the art is how to avoid them

queuing in the heat. Most of the grockles and day tourists head straight from Piazzale Roma bus station or the railway station, along the main drag past the Rialto Bridge to St Mark's Square and the Doge's Palace, and do not get much further than that.

So here we have it, a list of the 11 best places you should go and do, looking at why you should go, what you should do and see when you get there and how to best to do it, avoiding the crowds, being part of it and really enjoying the experience.

Some places, like Piazza San Marco, you have to see them, like it or not; but don't make it everything like most people do. A number of places places have no crowds, even in August. Venice is known to be expensive, but it doesn't have to be, many places are free. So, based on considered opinion, varied tastes of different people, cost, and a balanced cross section of interests, I have come up with the list below.

Unfortunately, most of the top sights come with crowds, but the art is how to avoid them and how to avoid

Leave the phones at home for a better experience

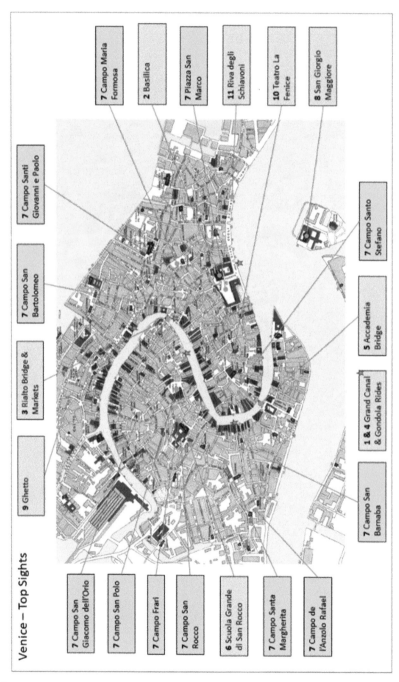

1   Go for a romantic ride in a gondola

Expensive

A gondola is a long sleek black boat sitting in the water slightly off centre; with its single oar worked by a professional gondolier. It looks like a cross between a canoe and a coffin, but it is neither, it is more like an expensive carriage which glides effortlessly down the Venice canals. Gondolas are unique to Venice; you will not find them anywhere else in the world.

Expensive it may be, but you have to do it, so as not to return

Just sheer magic gliding along the Grand Canal

Rialto Bridge at its best

home feeling very disappointed that you did not have this unique experience. You should be looking to set aside about €100, although there are cheaper ways. What is better than being serenaded by your gondolier, against the stunning backdrop of Baroque buildings, gliding under the Rialto Bridge, having an experience of your life you won't forget.

"Pretend it's Carnevale time, don a mask, or just a fresh shirt - and become someone else for a night." - Rick Steves. It's all part of living the dream, even if you do nothing else and live on cheap pizza. You will certainly be the centre of attention.

Here is someone else's thoughts. "I felt it was definitely the highlight of my visit to Venice and a gondola ride isn't just reserved for romantic dates. Since the canals are Venice's roads, you'll be sharing them with other boats and gondolas. But it's so worth it to rest your weary feet and see Venice from a different perspective, to the quiet sound of the paddle hitting the water".

In a romantic dream world, gliding through the local canals in the Cannaregio

There is a set rate, officially 40 mins for €80, and €100 after 7pm, but you need to negotiate and agree on the price and duration of the trip, as many a gondolier will not stick to it. Some can try and charge you double that, and accordions and singers are more. Time of day is also important; they get busier in the early evening.

Well, it is sort of romantic!!

There are alternatives. Share the cost as a group - a gondola will take up to 6 people. Or book as part of a package and let someone else do the negotiating for you. Check www.tripadvisor.com or book direct on sites like www.venicewelcome.com or www.localvenicetours.com.

A little acrobatic technique helps

So where is best to go and find a gondola station? If you go near St Mark's, the gondolas queue up under Bridge of Sighs and you share your space with everyone else - far from romantic. A suggestion, if you want a good experience, is to do a mixture of the backwater canals and the Grand Canal. If you go to one of the stations either side of the Rialto Bridge, you also get to go under this iconic masterpiece in a gondola too: Traghetto Riva del Carbon near the Rialto vaporetto stop or Traghetto Santa Sofia near the Ca' d'Oro stop. There are other smaller stations along the Grand Canal, or sometimes you just find a gondola waiting for a trip. Just wander around.

Day and night are both good. You may see more during the day, but night can be more romantic. At night, when the hordes of day trippers have gone, another Venice appears. Glide in a gondola through quiet canals while music echoes across the water from the restaurants and the bars.

TOP TIP: Don't get ripped off. Make sure you negotiate and agree a price before you go or it will go up.

TOP TIP: If cost is a consideration, choose your time of day and location away from St Mark's. It is worth considering sharing with others.

2 Basilica di San Marco, the most beautiful church in Italy

Open 09.45 to 17.00 Mon to Sat, 14.00 to 17.00 Sun. Free for 10 mins, €2 to €5 to stay longer and see more.

A visit to Basilica di San Marco is a must for a first-time tourist to Venice, as the church holds so many precious artworks and relics that you will not see anywhere else. It is the most famous and most beautiful church in Venice, and many consider it the most ostentatious church in Italy. It is also one of the finest examples of Byzantine architecture anywhere in the world. The gold interior is just stunning and oozes wealth from a bygone age.

The Basilica in St Mark's Square (with the pigeons!)

The gleaming Basilica overlooks Piazza San Marco and adjoins the Doge's Palace. It consists of an amazing ornate façade with many gargoyles, and is topped with a number of huge domes. Inside, even though it is quite dark, the gold interior just radiates such an intensity. Its impressive opulent design of gold ground mosaics, and its status as a symbol of Venetian wealth and power from the 11th century just screams out. The marble floor has a character of its own as it has shifted with the centuries of Venice's sinking history. And just look at the inside of the amazing domes.

Gleaming gold interior from the days of opulence

Admission to the Basilica is free, but visitors should expect to pay entrance fees during holidays or to special parts of the Basilica complex, such as the St Mark's museum, Pala d'Oro, the Bell Tower, and the Treasury. While admission to Basilica di San Marco may be free, it is restricted. Visitors are allowed approximately 10 minutes to walk through and admire the Basilica's beauty. Why spend only 10 minutes in the church after queuing for so much longer? It doesn't make sense.

Alternatively, it only costs €5 to go up to the balcony and see a terrific view of Piazza San Marco and the inside and outside of the Basilica in your own time. Also, paying to see the lavishly decorated altarpiece (Pala d'Oro) is worth it if you really like gold and

11

precious jewels. Beneath the altar is where the body of St Mark lies, and the altarpiece itself is laden with riches dating from the 10th century.

The queues at the Basilica can be long and painful, especially in July and August when it is hot outside and thousands of tourists abound. The tour companies all bowl up at around 11.00, jumping the queue and slowing it down. It is best to either arrive early and queue early or arrive after 3pm. Better still, you can skip the queue by purchasing online at a cost of €2.00 per

View from the Basilica balcony, well worth it

person (free for children up to 5 years old) to get privileged access to St Mark's Basilica and avoid the long line. To do this, see www.venetoinside.com. Also note that bags and cameras are no longer allowed in the Basilica; you have to leave them in lockers as directed from the security at the main doors.

If you want to visit the Basilica without crowds, you can attend a sung mass (9am Mon-Sat and 10.30am Sun).

Visitors are recommended to respect the sacred place, in particular, with appropriate dress code and being on best behaviour.

TOP TIP: It's more than worthwhile paying the €5 to see the Basilica in your own time.

TOP TIP: The upstairs balcony provides a grandstand view of Piazza San Marco - not to be missed.

The Grand Canal from the Rialto Bridge

12

3 Feel the bustling trading hub of old merchant Venice at the Rialto Bridge and Markets

Free

The Rialto Bridge is one of the world's most iconic bridges, and only one of four which have buildings on them. The others are Bath (Pulteney Bridge), Florence (Ponte Vecchio), and the Verana Bridge Restaurant on the Anshun Bridge, across the Jin River in Chengdu in China. More recently a fifth bridge has been added, Blackfriars station (London). The Rialto Bridge is also one of the best known sights in Venice, with classic views seen in many a painting and picture book.

The Grand Canal and Rialto Bridge

The Rialto Bridge

It was the first of four bridges built over the Grand Canal, by many years. The Rialto Bridge has spanned the canal at this location for centuries and connects the districts of San Polo, to the west, and San Marco, to the east. The first bridge at this crossing was an early pontoon bridge, later replaced by a wooden drawbridge of sorts. The current ornate bridge made of stone dates to the late 16th century. Following the building of the Rialto Bridge, three others were added. The Ponte dell'Accademia built as a steel bridge in 1854 and the Ponte degli Scalzi built in 1934. The Ponte dell'Accademia was replaced by a wooden bridge in 1933 and then again by another wooden bridge in 1985 (a reproduction of the deteriorating one from 1933). The last, and fourth, bridge over the Grand Canal, the Ponte della Costituzione, was built very recently near the station in 2008.

The shops on the Rialto Bridge aren't terribly exciting, they are mostly jewellers and souvenir shops. Nor are the crowds which throng over the bridge at prime time and get in your way as this is the main crossing and meeting point on the canal between the station and St Mark's Square. Better to climb the exterior sets of steps at the back of the shops, or head through the arches on the top of the bridge, then you can really admire the setting, with fine views over the Grand Canal, busy with gondolas, ferries and working boats.

The fish market early in the morning

The Rialto Bridge at night

Nearby are the city's markets, the fresh produce and the fish market, in Campo della Pescaria. The markets have been there for over 700 years and the fish market smells like it. This is the area where the first banks were established; traders who made Venice rich set sail from here and sold their goods on return; it is also where courts met, prisoners were held and punished, and new laws were declared.

The Rialto Markets are located at the north-west of the Rialto Bridge in the district of San Polo. The location is alongside the Grand Canal to the right behind the souvenir stalls. Venice's bustling Rialto Markets have been whetting appetites for centuries. Early in the morning, heavily laden workaday gondolas and boats, bulging with all sorts of goodies, deliver essential supplies. No lorries, no vans - this is the only way, as otherwise it is hard work manoeuvring everything up and down the narrow stairs of every bridge over every canal; so the boat is the only sensible choice.

The Rialto Markets – Fresh fruit from the Veneto

There you will see all kinds of exotic fish of all shapes, colours and sizes from the lagoon. Many restaurants get their fresh produce from here. Scour the stalls for glistening mountains of moscardini (baby octopus), moeche (soft-shell crabs), and inky seppie (squid). Sustainable fishing practices are not a new idea at the Pescaria, where marble plaques show regulations set centuries ago for minimum allowable sizes for lagoon fish. Locally caught seafood is tagged 'Nostrano', as are seasonal vegetables like Sant'Erasmo castraure (baby artichokes) and radicchio trevisano (bitter red chicory) at neighbouring stalls.

Chill out and feel the atmosphere of this market. Smell and feel the freshness of the local Mediterranean-grown products found everywhere, marvellous if you have an apartment and can take back a carrier bag full of vegetables for an al fresco dinner washed down with a bottle or two of best Italian vino rosso. The market closes at 2pm.

Amazing view of the Grand Canal from the bridge

14

Happily, there is still some authentic local atmosphere to be savoured. The little old ladies from Cannaregio cross the Grand Canal on the vaporetto or the little traghetto gondola with their shopping trolleys each morning. The markets are still a place where local people can shop for their daily food and goodies at reasonably low prices.

Otherwise, sit out on the steps and banks by the Rialto Markets and watch the people and boats go by, especially at night with a bottle of wine from the local supermarket, but be discreet as it may be illegal, but also much cheaper for those on a budget. A good supermarket is the one in Piazzale Roma next to the Grand Canal. Immerse yourself in the atmosphere and chill out, pretending you have gone back a century or two.

TOP TIP: Get up early and visit the Rialto Bridge when it belongs to the Venetians and the markets are at full steam, brimming with real local atmosphere, before the tourists arrive.

View from the vaporetto

4 Travel the Grand Canal at night, and watch silhouettes of the historic buildings glide by

Vaporetto, single ticket or use your pass

The Grand Canal cuts right through the centre of the city and divides it in two. Some of the best views of Venice are seen from the Grand Canal, day or night, including those from the steps of the Rialto Bridge (or Ponte di Rialto), and the Accademia Bridge looking towards St Mark's. Experiencing a trip on the Grand Canal at midnight will send excitement rushing through your veins.

Night lights from the Ponte degli Scalzi Bridge

Charming in daylight, Venice gains an aura of captivating mystery at night. A canal ride on a starry night is a unique experience that lasts for a lifetime. Romantic canal banks, bridges in various shapes and sizes, buildings glowing under the light of street lanterns all the way along the Grand Canal.

Take the vaporetto No. 1 all the way from St Mark's Square to the railway station or Piazzale Roma. Along the way you will see many of Venice's key sights including the Salute, the Palazzo Ca'Rezzonico and will pass under the Rialto Bridge.

There is nothing more magical than a full moon over the lagoon or Grand Canal at night. You will taste the atmosphere of gondolas serenading and music emerging from dimly lit bars and cafés as the boat glides by. It also offers great night time views of ornate ceilings and chandeliers inside the historic palazzi that line both sides of the canal.

15

Full moon over the Lagoon at St Mark's – Magical!

The best place to sit on the No. 1 and No. 2 vaporetto lines is outside at the back. These boats have sheltered outdoor seating areas in the stern (accessible through doors at the back of the passenger cabin) and on older boats in the bow. These seats are great for sightseeing, and you'll have the best chance of nabbing them if you board at the vaporetto a stop or two before St Mark's. The whole trip takes about 45 minutes and you see the whole Grand Canal and the Rialto Bridge in its full glory.

TOP TIP: For a night cruise get on before St Mark's, either at San Zaccaria Pieta or Arsenale station and sit at the back of the boat for the best view.

5   Accademia Bridge - see the classic view of the Santa Maria della Salute as the famous artists did centuries before

Free

The view from the Accademia Bridge is the scene of many famous paintings produced by the very famous artists including Canaletto, Turner and Monet. You can actually picture the same view as your ancestors. It offers two of the best views in Venice, both looking along the Grand Canal, one in each direction. On one side lies the dome of Santa

Accademia Bridge

Maria della Salute, and on the other is the quieter bend which eventually takes the canal towards the Rialto Bridge. These famous vistas have been illustrated all over the world, particularly the view of the Salute looking towards St Mark's and the Lagoon. Venice has inspired artists, poets and film makers throughout the centuries and the vision it has given them is embedded in many of their great works.

Santa Maria della Salute from the bridge

16

The Accademia Bridge is also a good place to view the Regatta, which starts at the Rialto and comes down the Grand Canal to the Lagoon. This bridge still has much more atmosphere than the other bridges. Local cafés and restaurants are found on both the Dorsoduro side and around Campo Santo Stefano, a couple of minutes away in the San Marco district. Like most of the gorgeous views in Venice, I could just stand here and look at it all day. The further you go from the bridge, the less crowded it gets.

Not much different from centuries ago

This view has not changed much in time either

TOP TIP: For dinner, try booking a waterside seat in Bar Foscarini, right at the base of the Accademia Bridge, facing this classic view of the Salute. It is probably the best table in the whole city.

TOP TIP: Visit the bridge early as it can get very crowded, especially in summer as it is the main crossing point between San Marco and the Dorsoduro.

Piazza San Marco

17

6   See grand works of art in the Scuola Grande di San Rocco

Open daily 09.30 to 17.30. Entry €10

The upstairs gallery

Venice is a mecca for old art and art lovers. It is full of many famous works and hidden treasures painted on the walls and ceilings of many of the churches and palaces.

The Scuola Grande di San Rocco is one of the best, a unique site where over 60 paintings of Jacopo Tintoretto are preserved in their original setting in a building that has hardly undergone any alteration since its construction. In the impressive main hall, from ceiling to floor, virtually every space contains a different artwork. Dedicated to the patron saint of the plague, Scuola Grande di San Rocco was one of the many great religious schools throughout Venice. The architecture of the building is as impressive as the paintings. If for no other reason, it is a must see.

If you are into art, there is a €10 charge to visit Rocco, but it's worth every cent. The ceilings are magnificent and marble and art work are definitely worth exploring. There are many sites in Venice you don't have to pay for but this place is the exception. Don't forget to pick up the mirrors at the end of the hall to save your neck when viewing the paintings on the ceiling, though they are pretty heavy - slipped discs beware. Also admire the wooden statues that can easily be missed in the splendour of everything else.

A bit of history in how the paintings originated. The paintings in the Scuola Grande di San Rocco were painted by Tintoretto. To gain the commission, he cheated. Instead of producing sketches of his proposed works like other artists, he gifted a magnificent ceiling panel of the patron St Roch, which he knew could not be refused. The artist documents Mary's life story in the assembly hall, and both Old and New Testament scenes in the Sala Grande Superiore upstairs. When Tintoretto painted these works, Venice's outlook was grim indeed: the plague had taken 50,000 Venetians, including the great colourist Titian.

Campo San Rocco

TOP TIP: If you are into art or not into art or are an old art lover this place is a must see. It will mesmerise you and is worth every cent of the €10 entry fee.

Campo San Vio, Dorsoduro

7   Piazzas and Campos

Free

Campo dei Frari

There are many piazzas and campos (squares) in Venice, in fact 127 of them. The most well know are Piazza San Marco and Piazzale Roma. Piazza San Marco is a must, but Piazzale Roma is really a bus station where the majority of tourists arrive at the end of the causeway and is outside the historic city. Unless you are into buses and crowds, there is not much else to see here.

Most of the tourists head for Piazza San Marco; it is beautiful but it can get very crowded, and one may be disappointed as with all those people and their grot, it can look a bit scruffy and grubby, which takes some of the charm away compared with many other campos in city. Take away the people, the rubbish and the pigeons, it looks much better, like 6am in the picture opposite

Piazza San Marco – place to your self at sunrid

In origin, campo means field and many are beautiful open spaces, almost always located in front of a church and therefore paved. When you come into a campo, it is a relief from the claustrophobic alleyways and lack of sunlight, especially in winter. Many have wellheads which were essential to the survival of the local people. The campos are lively meeting places extremely valued by Venetians, young and old, and are in effect playgrounds where the young Venetians play football or ride their bikes, even if it is forbidden in Venice.

The leaning tower from Campo Sant'Angelo

As well as being more aesthetic and rustic, many of the campos are much quieter with fewer people than St Mark's. They have shops and cafés with a more community feel and local ambiance. Venetians are quite social people and love to meet and talk.

Top 11 Sights at a Glance

Here is a list of some of the best a look at:

Campo Santo Stefano, San Marco. Once the city's main market square, Santo Stefano is an expansive place, full of less expensive restaurants and cafés around the Santo Stefano church, only 10 minutes from St Mark's.

Campo Santo Stefano

Coffee stop - Campo Santa Margherita

Campo Santa Margherita, Dorsoduro. A lively market square during the day, with a delicious bakery and trees to eat under while feeding birds. After sunset Campo Santa Margherita has a great sense of ambiance being the focus of Venetian nightlife, restaurants, bars, at the centre of the Dorsoduro.

Campo Santa Maria Formosa, Castello. A working market square dominated by the Baroque-dressed parish church and one of the best campos in the city. A bridge leads to the Fondazione Querini Stampalia, a house full of magnificent treasures, one of the best preserved houses in Europe.

Campo Santa Maria Formosa

Campo San Barnaba

Campo San Barnaba, Dorsoduro. A charming square dominated by its church with a canal on one side and gondolas gliding by. In the film *Indiana Jones and the Last Crusade* (1989), the church (only the exterior) was used as the setting for an imaginary library. The Campo San Barnaba, in front of the church, was then used to shoot the scene in which the protagonist of the film, after having

passed through the (non-existent) underground passages in search of the tomb of one of the keepers of the Holy Grail knights, emerges out of a manhole in the middle of the square, to the embarrassment of the elegant clients of the bar seated at the tables.

Campo San Polo, Santa Croce. A large square dominated by its church and the well in the centre. This is also the place where many of the carnivals are held. It is usually quiet in the evening and a good place for a stroll.

Campo San Polo – large open space

Campo San Giacomo dell'Orio, Santa Croce. More of a local feel of Venice fully alive in this delightful square. Local children playing games in the campo while parents chat in cafés, with washing strung out across alleys. What remains so special about San Giacomo is that it is a place where local residents rather than tourists still set the tone.

Campo San Giacomo dell'Orio

Campo San Bartolomeo

Campo San Bartolomeo, San Marco. Tucked away next door to the Rialto Bridge, full of life with shops, cafés and street bars.

Campo de l'Anzolo Rafael, Dorsoduro. A quiet square, often empty, and happily overshadowed by the Chiesa dell'Angelo Raffaele with its twin campanile. Although the campo seems isolated, there are shops and nice restaurant with access via a vaporetto stop (San Basilio) close by.

Campo de l'Anzolo Rafael

Campo San Rocco

Campo San Rocco, Santa Polo. A small square surrounded by beautiful buildings. Home of the famous gallery. Also a good gelato bar with no queue.

Campo Santi Giovanni e Paolo, Castello. This is a large open attractive square next to the hospital, dominated by its church, which is worth visiting and a large statue of a horse, if you like horses.

What also makes the campos particularly attractive in Venice is the feeling of space that they make available. After trying to find your way through the narrow and tortuous calli (alleys), if you are lost, to arrive on a big campo such as that of

Campo Santi Giovanni e Paolo

22

Santa Margherita or Santo Stefano is always a pleasure and a relief - the space and light ... and you now know where you are again! Venice suddenly seems much bigger.

TOP TIP: Regularly rest those weary feet. Spend time in a café in one of the campos and watch the world go by and the locals socialise.

8   View of Venice from the tower of San Giorgio Maggiore

Open daily 08.30 to 20.00. Entry to the tower €6, the church is free

The tower of San Giorgio Maggiore provides spectacular views of Venice without the queues for the Campanile in St Mark's Square. It is only 5 minutes from St Mark's by No. 2 vaporetto, where you can see it just across the Lagoon. From the top, you can see St Mark's, the Basilica and the Doge's Palace.

View overlooking St Mark's from San Giorgio Maggiore

The church is worth seeing too. It is church in the classical renaissance style and its brilliant white marble gleams above the blue water of the lagoon opposite the Piazza and forms the focal point of the view from every part of the Riva degli Schiavoni. It was a monastery at one time. The church is imposing from outside and most impressive inside, and houses two very large paintings by Tintoretto.

The high point is the trip to the top of the campanile which is well worth the ride and the views give a new perspective on Venice.

Giudecca

At €6, the lift to the top is also cheaper than St Mark's, and is well worth the money. Even though the queues are not as lengthy at St Mark's, it is best to go early morning or late afternoon. But one thing to be aware of, if you are up there on the hour when the bells go off, they will scare the living daylights out of you, so hang on tight.

TOP TIP: Spend time seeing the church too.

TOP TIP: Get the vaporetto the short hop to the next island of Giudecca and walk along the front with a grandstand view of Venice.

23

9 Ghetto - Venice from a different perspective

Free

The Ghetto is a little different from the other areas of Venice. It is a remarkable place flanked by high-rise late medieval buildings. It even has kosher restaurants. The Venetian Ghetto dates from 1516 when the Doge decreed that all Jews were to live in a small gated and curfewed city island, separated from the rest of Venice. The gates were unlocked at dawn and locked by sunset and all residents were required to wear yellow headgear or a badge. There were doctors, moneylenders, merchants,

Campo Ghetto

and villains like Shakespeare's Shylock (Merchant of Venice). By 1797 disease, war and politics had shrunk the population of the ghetto to 3,000. Napoleon's troops brought an end to the Republic of Venice and to the Ghetto; they burned down the gates, and French principles of liberty, equality and fraternity allowed the Ghetto's inhabitants at last to be free and equal.

Campo del Ghetto Nuovo still feels like a place apart. Due to lack of space, the houses were built taller than in the rest of Venice to increase the amount of accommodation. Small rooms and overcrowding led to cramped squalid conditions. There are still synagogues here;

The Ghetto, early morning, out walking the dog

for example, there is one on the top floor of the nine-storey buildings which surround the campo. Also there is a Holocaust museum in an unexpected campo laced with a haunting history.

The Cannaregio canals

Two other places to see are Campo dell'Abbazia and its herringbone floor and, on the opposite side of the canal, the Scuola Vecchia della Misericordia; the original seat of the Scuola was built in the Gothic style from 1308 onwards, where it still stands today

Local people in the campo

The Ghetto is a much more peaceful place than the main sights and just as attractive. That alone makes it a must to see. The Ghetto is made up of Campo Ghetto Nuovo itself and three peaceful parallel canals. It has much more of a local community feel with small shops and cafés. A good place to chill out with a coffee and feel more integrated with the locals. This is the real Venice.

24

TOP TIP: To see all three canals do a bit of one and cross over to another. You will need to do a double take as they all look the same.

10   Teatro La Fenice

Open daily 09.30 to 18.00. Entry €9

Teatro La Fenice is one of the most famous and renowned landmarks in the history of Italian theatre and in the history of opera as a whole. Especially in the 19th century, La Fenice became the venue of many famous operatic premieres at which the works of several of the four major bel canto era composers - Rossini, Bellini, Donizetti and Verdi - were performed.

Teatro La Fenice – Inside

On 29 January 1996, La Fenice was completely destroyed by fire. Only its acoustics were preserved, because Lamberto Tronchin, an Italian acoustician, had measured the acoustics two months earlier. Following the fire it reopened for the first performance in December 2003.

Even if you are not into theatre or opera, you should go there just to see the stunning architecture of the interior. There are a whole variety of shows from musical concerts to opera, just check it out on the La Fenice website for the latest programme of events, http://www.teatrolafenice.it.

TOP TIP: Always book well in advance so as not to be disappointed.

Teatro La Fenice – Outside

11   Stroll along the Riva degli Schiavoni and see the Bridge of Sighs

Free

The Riva degli Schiavoni is one of the world's greatest promenades built in the 9th century and named after the Slavic men who brought cargo to the city from across the Adriatic Sea. Centuries ago vessels would dock and disembark here, and you could hear different languages as traders, dignitaries and sailors arrived from around the Mediterranean hoping to sell their wares.

Bridge of Sighs

Riva degli Schiavoni – long promenade

One of the highlights of Venice is a walk along this waterfront promenade. This is what Venetians do best. During the summer months, it is very busy in the day with souvenir vendors, but very quiet at night for a peaceful stroll. Venetians also stroll along the Zattere which runs along the front of the Dorsoduro.

While walking along the promenade, you will pass the Hotel Danieli. Even though most of us cannot afford to stay there, have a quick look inside - you will be completely taken aback by the reception area and main hall of the hotel. 50 meters down the canal, beside the Doge's Palace, is the Bridge of Sighs. This was the one-way entry into the prison, so you may not wish to stay there. It was not a nice place.

These days the sea front is full of pleasure boats, rather than boats from distant lands. While you are meandering along, pause for a while to take a photo of the gondolas in front of you bobbing up and down in the waters of the lagoon. Also take in views of the Island of San Giorgio Maggiore opposite, with its magnificent Palladian architecture that dominates the skyline; the designer was a famous architect and just loved height and grandeur. You have just become part of the classic views of Venice which you will remember for the rest of your life.

TOP TIP: Stroll down to the Arsenale and get the boat back up the Grand Canal. The further you go, the less crowded it gets.

The Riva Degli Schiavoni – boats coming and going

Some other ideas...

There are plenty of other things to do in Venice, many which will add to your experience and memories to take back home. Here are a few more:

- Arrive in style, either a trip across Europe on the Orient Express or a private water taxi from the airport. Expensive it may be, but you may never do it again.
- Rest those weary feet, take a trip around the outside of the main island and see Venice from the outside in, either vaporetto No.4 or No.5. They go round in opposite directions.
- Get up early before breakfast and go for a stroll with the place to yourself and

Van man on the Grand Canal – the only way to get the stuff moved around here

26

maybe see the reflection of the palaces in the Grand Canal while the water is still. With no one around the place will look like a film set ready for an action movie, like James Bond in *Casino Royale* or many others which have been created here. Maybe see the sun rise at St Mark's Square come up over the lagoon.

- Again, get up early and see a different side of the city with Venetians going about their business before the tourists arrive.
- Lagoon and other islands. For a longer stay, see San Michele (cemetery), Burano and Torcello. If you like the beach, the Lido is worth a look, but it is typically modern 20th century architecture, standard hotels and no tourist sights.
- Palaces and palazzos. Venice was built out of palaces, particularly along the Grand Canal. Many of these are open to the public as museums, art galleries or to show you how people lived in a bygone age.

Fresh food everywhere - Campo San Barnaba

- Children. There is plenty for children to do in Venice, see Chapter 4

- **FREE Venice.** Many things in Venice are free, including some of the Top 11 Sights listed above. Often the free things are best. Here are some others, it just takes a little imagination:
  - o State-owned museums are free on the first Sunday of each month.
  - o Churches: many of them are free and have wonderful works of art and architecture, always worth poking your nose in if you are passing by. You never know what you will find.
  - o Sit and chill out and watch the boats go by; there is always plenty going on, especially early in the morning when all the deliveries arrive.
  - o Isola di San Michele Cemetery.
  - o Concerts in churches and halls: check the web and posters for what is currently going on.

Canal side cafés everywhere – San Marco

Whatever you end up doing, chill out and enjoy yourself, there is always a lot going on.

Just walk along the waterfront - Zattere from Giudecca

Just living the dream

Chapter 3 - Making the Most of It

![The first sight of Venice many visitors get of Venice]

The first sight of Venice many visitors get of Venice

A trip to Venice does not have to be as daunting a prospect as you might think, and with a little bit of pre-thought and planning you will have a much more enjoyable experience. Most people don't plan, they just arrive and switch into headless chicken mode at Piazzale Roma and miss a lot of the best things in the process. The trick, from an experienced traveller, is to keep a plan as simple as possible, and don't over-plan. The result of over-planning is that when things don't work out perfectly or as perceived, it can stress you out and often leads to disappointment and can ruin the trip. It also leaves little room for life's myriad unexpected events to just happen and fun memories that may result.

To help make life easier and get you started, we cover some of the basic things you need to consider to make the most of it, from getting there, where to stay and how to get around. Also, Venice does not have to be expensive. The general rule of thumb is that the nearer you are to St Mark's Square, the higher the price, the bigger the crowds and the lower the quality, particularly where cafés and restaurants are concerned.

Before you go

Before you go, have an idea of how long you want to stay for, what you want to see and do, and finally find where everything is located on the map. That will make it much easier deciding the best area and place to stay, seeing what places are close together and doing it in a joined-up fashion rather than racing backwards and forwards wasting a lot time unnecessarily darting around. So here is a simple list that may help make it easier when you get there:

Just a beautiful place to go

- How long? Many people only spend a day, but 4 days, 3 nights is best, allowing for travel too.

29

- When? Are you good with crowds or not good with crowds? Venice gets very busy in the summer, but there are quieter times to go. May and September are better if you still want good weather.
- Have an idea of what you want to see and make an outline plan so you don't waste time doing this when you get there. Get an A4 map and mark everything on it so you know where all the places are. It is easier doing this using the internet; and make a copy so it doesn't matter if you ruin one in the rain or

Many canals and beautiful views to see – Murano

from having it in your pocket. Do you like museums or hate galleries? Do you want to see the main sights as described in the previous chapter, do you like architecture and old buildings? Or have you come for the food?
- So just read up a bit on Venice so you know what to expect and find it more interesting when you get there. Many people have the misconception it is an overcrowded cruise ship destination, a ghost town of sorts, but that is not the case. There is more to see and do than just crowds. 56,000 locals still live there.

Getting there

Art in glass – Murano

Getting to Venice is easy. The main options are air, rail, road and boat.

Air. There are two airports, Marco Polo and Treviso. The majority of the flights arrive at Marco Polo, while the budget airlines tend to use Treviso. Marco Polo is much nearer with a more regular bus or boat service to the city: about 20 minutes, €8 per person by bus one way or €25 by shared water taxi. Private water taxis are much more expensive. From Treviso, the journey time is about 70 minutes and €15 one way per person. Also, the bus service is less frequent. For either journey it is best to buy a return ticket which is valid for up to 10 days.

Rail. Venice station is on the main Italian intercity rail network with many fast trains, including a direct service from Milan; and there is the Orient Express for those who want to arrive in style. The station is right in the city at the end of the Causeway. From here it is easy to walk or catch a vaporetto to your hotel from the stops just outside the main entrance.

Vaporettos go everywhere. The Giudecca Canal

Road. Venice can easily be reached by both car and coach. The main dropping off point is at Piazzale Roma at the end of the Causeway. This is also where the main carparks are, Tronchetto parking island, as you can go no further. There are no roads in Venice. For parking, you are looking at between €21 and €30 a day. There is cheaper car parking at Mestre station on the mainland, at €10 a day, and then it is 12 minutes by train. Also, there are a number of secure garages in Mestre. An alternative is the San Giuliano car parks on the outskirts of Mestre, next to the Venetian Lagoon. Parkers can take a water bus to Venice in 24 minutes for less than the cost of a vaporetto ride in the city centre.

Tram. There is a tram system from Mestre to the railway station and Piazzale Roma. See http://www.urbanrail.net/eu/it/venezia/venezia-mestre.htm for map of stations and stops.

Boat. Most people who arrive by boat come on a cruise ship, one of those monsters that dwarfs everything around them and that will moor up at the cruise terminal near Piazzale Roma. Venice is also serviced by long-distance ferries from other areas of Italy and countries on the Adriatic. More local is the extended vaporetto service from local towns and islands; see 'Getting around' below. Some cruise lines run free buses to Piazzale Roma, but they are not always advertised.

People Mover. Elevated shuttle trains offer quick (and wheelchair-accessible) connections between three points on the edge of the city's historic centre.

Beautiful backwaters

- Piazzale Roma, where locals and visitors arrive in the city by public bus, airport bus, taxi, or car.
- The Marittima cruise terminal, where many passenger ships arrive and depart. The Marittima station is located just outside the Marittima port entrance, which means that passengers still need to walk to or from their ships.
- Tronchetto parking island, which has indoor and outdoor parking for thousands of cars and is also the arrival point for most tour buses.

A single fare between any two points is €1.50.

How long to stay

Depending on how long you have, the optimum stay is around 4 days and 3 nights. This will give you time to see the best of the city without rushing around. But if you only have a day, this is more than possible and you can still have a great time. Later chapters cover suggested itineraries for both day trips and longer stays, and how to make the most of your time here whichever you choose.

The Danieli, well maybe!! – Castello

Where to stay

There are many options for where to stay, from further afield and making a day trip of it, to staying in the city itself. There are cheaper hotels with parking just across the Causeway on the mainland. But if you want to really experience the ambiance and atmosphere of Venice, my view is to stay in the city. It may be more expensive, but in most cases it is more than worth it and much nicer too. Also, if you need to have a rest from all the walking around, it is much easier to have a room nearby in your hotel to crash out in or to be able to go for an early morning or evening walk when the city is much quieter.

Rialto Markets – The big people used to stay here

As for where to stay, there are a whole range for hotels depending on your budget, from the very expensive Hotel Danieli or Gritti Palace to much more reasonable, including some less salubrious abodes. Bear in mind, if you have heavy luggage or awkward suitcases, there are lots of stairs, so it is best to be near a vaporetto stop. Location can be important. It is also recommended to reduce the size of your luggage, as there is a maximum size you can take on the vaporetto. Elton J or Posh Spice would certainly struggle.

The best deals normally combine a flight and hotel, but it is always a good idea to check where the hotel is and how good it is using review sites like TripAdvisor.

The nearer you are to St Mark's Square or the Grand Canal, the more expensive and crowded it gets. There are quieter places in the Cannaregio or Ghetto area, but then it is much further to walk to the rest of the sights in the city.

One suggestion which I have found works well is to stay near the Grand Canal in the old city up near the station in the Santa Croce area. This is near the No.1 vaporetto, a good option for getting around, and much cheaper than near St Mark's Square. Also, you get a hands-on view of the Grand Canal at midnight on your way back if you are a habitual stop-out. It is also quicker and easier to drop your luggage off when you arrive.

More ideas on accommodation and how best to find the place of your dreams are given in Chapter 10.

TOP TIP. Half of the experience of Venice is seeing it at night. It may be a little more expensive, but it does pay to stay on the island.

TOP TIP. Keep your luggage to a minimum as there are lots of stairs and few porters, and there is a maximum size permitted on the vaporetto.

What's going on round here then? Local resident in Campo San Polo

TOP TIP. Having your hotel near a vaporetto stop makes it much easier to find your way back at night.

Getting around

There are two ways to get around Venice, on foot or by boat along the canals. There are no roads and no Uber, just water taxis, which are expensive, or the cheaper vaporetto service. Walking means lots of stairs to climb the bridges over the canals together with a lot of map reading. Boats only go up and down the Grand Canal or round the island. You should do a bit of both. Unfortunately, Venice is not friendly for bicycles (they are banned), pushchairs, skateboards or wheelchairs. One has to blame

San Giorgio Maggiore

the 6th century designers for that. If you need wheelchair access, you need to plan in advance or take someone along with you who has big muscles and plenty of patience. Finding your way around the city is both exciting and daunting; it is a little confusing, can be difficult to work out and easy to lose direction. Venice is like a rabbit warren or maze you cannot cheat at, depending on how you view it. So for starters, you need a good map - like the ones in this book - not a bad one. Then you need to learn how to use it or it will be even more of a challenge finding your way.

One way to cross the Grand Canal

Walking will enable you to stop and start and take it all in. But it is tiring. Best to have lots of coffee or beer stops, and sit by the water or in a piazza café and watch the world go by. The key is to take your time, don't rush. This is a time to be lazy and chill out.

33

Just chilling out

To maximise your visit and make it easier to do more, later chapters in this book provide some example itineraries and walks in each area which all join up if you want to do the whole lot. They will show you an efficient way to get around the city and see the key sights.

Many people think they will not need to use the boat, but a vaporetto is the only way to cross the Grand Canal other than the major bridges, but in most cases the nearest bridge is always a long walk from where you happen to be. That's the way it works, as there are only four such bridges - three at the ends and only one in the middle. A trip on the boat is also a good way to rest those weary feet and go on a bit of an excursion.

Depending on how long you are staying, the most economical way is to buy a 1-day or 3-day vaporetto ticket as it is quite expensive doing it in single journeys. But remember to time stamp (validate) your ticket in the machine when you first use it or the boat inspectors will time stamp you with a very large fine.

Lots of narrow alleys – Dorsoduro

ACTV Vaporetto tickets can be purchased at most of the large vaporetto stations or at the Venezia Unica ticket offices or agencies in the historic centre and on the mainland. Also, they can be obtained from the network of authorised retailers that display the adhesive ACTV / Venezia Unica sticker.

A single, one-hour vaporetto trip in one direction costs €7.50 for any visitor aged 6 years and over. There are no discounts for seniors. A person in a wheelchair and their carer can travel for €1.50 per trip. Apart from these exceptions, everyone pays full fare unless a transport pass is used. This can be a much better deal. Each day runs for 24 hours from the time you validate the ticket. The cost of travel cards are as follows:

- €20.00 - 1 day travel card
- €30.00 - 2 days travel card
- €40.00 - 3 days travel card
- €60.00 - 7 days travel card

Hotels – Grand Canal, Santa Croce

TOP TIP. Staying in a hotel near a vaporetto stop is a good idea.

TOP TIP. Save money and your feet by getting a vaporetto pass for as many days you are in Venice. Also, you get straight on without queuing for a ticket.

One sister to another

Walks

To help you get around Venice, there are a number of suggested walks in later chapters: one to do Venice in a day and others which go around each of the four main areas. Following them will maximise both the experience and the time you have to spend, with plenty of interesting sights on the way, which should include something for everyone, except the most miserable who have an exception to walking anyway. The walks do have approximate times on them, but you need to add the time you spend seeing the sights en route and chilling out with a beer or two in bars. Also, some of us are slower than others and on less of a mission. Maybe it is possible to design an app to see if you are on target.

You will not have time to do everything suggested, so you will need to choose those things which interest you most. But generally, the time suggested does allow for a lot of stopping to look at things, take photographs and more. Each walk should be achievable in a day to allow you time off for good behaviour in enjoying the evening somewhere in a nice restaurant or a café alfresco with a bottle of vino.

Island of Murano

Quieter places

Venice can get very crowded, especially in July and August, when it can become really unbearable and hot in the wrong places. But don't despair, I have been there in August and had a great time and found deserted places. Also early morning and later in the evening when the day trippers have gone home is a good time.

Some of the quieter places you might like to try are:

- Dorsoduro, the western end between Campo Santa Margherita and the San Basilio vaporetto stop, going as far as the church at San Nicolo dei Mendicoli. Even in August during the day you will find very few people down that way. There are some lovely alleys and restaurants dotted about in this area and also the view of the Lagoon along the Zattere is magnificent.
- Cannaregio, the canals leading east from the Ghetto, very much more of a local feel and ambiance.

Not so many tourists here – San Polo

- Giudecca, walk along this island from one end to the other starting at the Sacca Fisola vaporetto stop to Zielle or vice versa. It's a lovely walk with bars and restaurants en route.

My advice to everyone who is hesitant in travelling to Venice is to get lost. I mean, get really lost. The city is like a maze and once you get away from the touristy areas and wander off the beaten track, you can immerse yourself in the peace and solitude surrounded by beautiful scenery. Go with no agenda except to fall in love with the city and I can promise you, you will do just that, if you allow yourself. Make it an adventure, not a mission.

Eating and drinking

Coffee houses everywhere

Cafés are part of the Venetian culture, many of them located in stunning piazzas or alongside canals. A visit to Venice would be missing if you did not sample the excellent coffee and, for those who want to indulge, the amazing pastries on offer.

There are also plenty of restaurants and bars everywhere. Some can get crowded so it's better either to book in advance or to eat a little bit earlier. Many tend to look derelict until they open up in the evening. Some are very expensive like Harry's Bar, an iconic drinking establishment near St Mark's (and there is also no beer here!), but as you move away from St Mark's Square and off the beaten track you will find many restaurants which will suit all sorts of tastes, budgets and fussy eaters. Have a wander round and make a choice. That is the hard part, there are so many to choose from.

There is more information on restaurants, cafés and bars in Chapter 10.

Shopping

Lots of stuff to buy

Venice is full of shops, some very posh and expensive and many others full of cheap tourist junk. Some things may be expensive, but Venice is full of wonderful things if you leave a little room in your hand luggage to take them home. More on shopping in Chapter 10.

TOP TIP. Even learning a few basic words in Italian will get you a long way with jaded shop keepers and restaurateurs. Trying is the most important part and you will see a huge difference in service compared with those who don't bother.

Tourist information

Zattere

There are 7 tourist offices run by the tourist authority of the province of Venice (namely, APT Venezia). These are located both in Venice (the lagoon) and in its mainland surroundings, in key areas like San Marco, the airport and Piazzale Roma. As well as the useful information they can give to visitors, they also offer free maps to help visitors get better oriented. They also sell and do deals including multi-entry Museum Passes (useful in particular if you are going into lots of them). They can also do deals and arrange gondola trips and many other types of organised tours with dining, to take even more €s off you.

See more at: http://www.venezia-tourism.com/en/tourist-information-offices-in-venice.html#sthash.Szce5e7h.dpuf

Grand Canal and Ponte degli Scalzi Bridge

37

Canale di Cannaregio

Chapter 4 – Venice in a Day

What is the art of the possible?

It may be impossible to see Venice in a day, but it is possible to see a lot of it in a day, as long as you make it a long one. It will all depend on what you want to do and see, your reason for coming and whether you have been to Venice before. Maybe you're on your own, with a group just sightseeing, you have a particular reason, or just want to chill out in bars. Or maybe you're on a date where you need to impress an important lady and not mess up.

Sunrise at St Mark's Square

Whatever the reason, it's worth thinking about it before you arrive. There is plenty to do and see. Here are some suggestions:

- For a first-time visit, see as many of the main sights as possible. You need to be able to move fast, as there are a lot of them. Be prepared to be exhausted; or it may be better to go a bit slower over a longer visit to take it all in.
- See old historic buildings and architecture. There are lots of them.
- Take photographs. There are plenty of photogenic scenes and classic vistas from the past to choose from and take home for memories.
- Bars, restaurants and cafés. Cafés are best, they really do have an ambiance, which is what the old Venetians did best and many still do.
- Museums. There are so many you won't have time to get around them in a day.

Splendid colours – San Polo

39

- Events. There are many of them, regattas, concerts, carnivals. It is best to look at the web as to what is currently going on.
- Boat trip or a gondola, both are a must, especially the latter if you have plenty of cash.
- Markets. There are a few, but the Rialto is the one, a special place; but you need to get there early as by lunch time it is all over.
- Or just wander and get lost. The best idea of all.

King Canute in the Grand Canal

And there is a lot more, but it is possible to have a go at all of the above in a day. The suggested itinerary in this chapter will show you round and enable you to achieve as much as possible in a relaxed way, and also have some fun too. You will get to see the main sights in a joined-up route without wasting time going backwards and forwards, and hopefully missing some of the crowds and avoiding a lot of queuing.

As I said, you can't do everything, but there should be something of interest for everybody. The idea is that you go at you own pace and pick the things which interest you. Do as little or as much as you want, stop off at a café or a bar for a beer, or lunch, it all works. This itinerary also allows you to divert off and do other things. The important thing is you are your own boss, you do what you want, when you want, see what you want, and spend as much time as you want.

Beautiful old buildings

An alternative option is to go on an arranged tour with a guide and a crowd of disparate people all on a schedule. Follow the flag! You have to behave, move on when you are told to, cannot wander off to look at something interesting (or you get put on the naughty step like I do), and very often have to listen to a monotonic broadcast of information overload until your ears are ringing and your mind switches off to cope. It depends on how interesting the guide is. Also, you can't have the experience of getting lost, but can still fall into the canal. It happens quite often. Which is better?

TOP TIP: Do Venice yourself and you will have a fantastic day.

A day trip to remember

A day in Venice should be a good day you remember for the rest of your life or you haven't done something right somewhere along the line.

However you travel to Venice, either on a cruise ship, a bus tour, car or train, most people coming for the day arrive in Piazzale Roma. That is the starting point, except for those arriving at the airport and staying longer, a few who use the water taxi direct to their hotel.

It may be impossible to see Venice in a day, but the suggested itinerary below gets you round a lot including most of the main

Cafés everywhere – San Marco

40

Calm waters at the Rialto Bridge

sights. The total walking time is about 3.5 hours, plus the time spent at each stop. So, 7 to 10 hours in total, allowing time for stopping off and seeing things and bite to eat. You will need to be the judge as you go along the route to see how well you are doing. It also works if you spread it over two days.

What should a day in Venice be like, what excites you, what are your objectives, what do you want to achieve by the end of the day? The first thing is that it should be stress free and relaxed. That takes time and patience rather than our customary rat-race mindset, so you don't overdo it. Fancy strolling along hand in hand sharing each other's company along the Zattere or Riva degli Schiavoni, or wandering through the streets of beautiful architecture, seeing amazing views from picture books in the real with a trip in a gondola. How fantastic is that. Live a dream.

After starting at Piazzale Roma, you should be on your way by now, seeing the wonder of the Grand Canal, looking with awe at the interior of the Frari, the artworks in the Scuola Grande di San Rocco and over bridges to the Campo Santa Margherita.

Canals in the Cannaregio

TOP TIP: Before you set off, you are here now, no more stress, deep breath, big smile, and relax. Take it steady. Slow is good.

Stopping off for a morning coffee and a pastry is a must, if you can fit it in (in both senses of the term); sit outside a café overlooking one of the amazing piazzas and watch the people go by. Maybe lunch in a canal-side bistro or in a hidden garden where there are many surprises which open up at meal times. Have some chill-out time to savour the experiences and gastronomies of the local cuisine.

Music on the Riva degli Schiavoni

After a short stroll along the Zattere, you head for the Accademia Galleries and the Bridge. If you are still feeling energetic, you can wander the couple of hundred metres or so into Campo Stefano for a beer or two. Otherwise, if your feet are now feeling the pace, time for a gondola or boat trip to the Salute, which is the centrepiece of many a classic painting.

A hop across the Grand Canal brings you to amazing views of Piazza San Marco and the lagoon. Hopefully by this time the crowds will have reduced and there will be less of a queue at the Basilica. If you have time, you can stroll along the Riva degli Schiavoni and see the Bridge of Sighs

From here it is a short distance from the posh shops of San Marco via the shopping streets of the Merceria to the Rialto Bridge. But men's wallets beware, keep your credit cards well hidden or leave them in the hotel.

Stroll along the Zattere

Now you have seen many of the main sights, have a look round the Rialto Markets and find a restaurant for something to eat. There are plenty to choose from round here with many beside the Grand Canal, ideal for a romantic candlelit dinner of local fish washed down with a bottle of vino or two.

Once you have found your legs again, it's a few metres stroll to the Rialto vaporetto stop (depending on the vino) to take the No.1 back to the station or Piazzale Roma, wherever you started.

What a day. You will have seen a lot, done a lot, and had a wonderful experience of this beautiful city.

Shopping at the Rialto Markets

Taking children to Venice

Depending on your point of view, this may or may not be a good idea. Children don't do culture till they get much older. But if you remember the basic premise that children think differently from adults and have a shorter attention spans than adults (some may say there is not much difference), it will be a good education for them and you will get along fine. In essence, children like doing rather than listening to tour guides or looking at static exhibits for hours. They don't like too much walking, don't appreciate the finer points of

Children like to play – Santa Croce

architecture or fine art, and don't like exotic cuisine and drawn-out meals, regardless of how much it costs. They get bored easily.

Venice, with its unfenced canals and open bridges, can be a nightmare for the health and safety experts. But other than strong reins needed for an unruly toddler, very few of them fall in the canal; it is usually the adult giving advice that does.

But there is plenty to do, and it is all about getting them involved. Venice is like an enormous playground. Go on the vaporetto, they will love that. Let them watch all the boating activity on the Grand Canal, they will like that too.

Football in the Ghetto

Feed them on the best Italian Margherita pizza, they will like that even better. And they won't say no to a big gelato.

Here are some other ideas:

- Palazzo Ducale. Some children do gruesome, it captures their imagination. Try the dungeons and some of the horrors of past generations.

Two on a bike!

- Gelato. Some of the best ice cream in the world will always go down well.
- Watching boats. This can keep children amused for hours, they like things which move and have action rather than the passive or still art.
- Trip around the island. Make good use of the vaporetto pass and take a trip on the No.4 or No.5 and do a complete circuit of the main city.
- Parks with play areas. Giardini Pubblici in the Castello is free and has a children's playground.
- Climbing towers. Try the Campanile in St Mark's or the church of San Giorgio Maggiore; see Chapter 2.
- See a glass works in action. Watch incredible pieces of artwork being made.
- Fondazione Querini Stampalia, an ancient and noble palace has a water garden and a children's area, as well as a café. The children's area (ages 3 to 6) is supervised: €5 for 2 hours from 13.00 to 18.00.
- Hidey holes. Children love these and there are plenty of them around the narrow alleys. Make it into a story, so they envision the past.

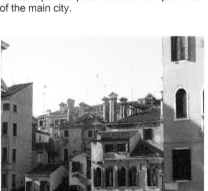

Look up as well as down, see those beautiful chimneys – Campo della Maddalena

- If in doubt, ask them; it may seem obvious, but stop at what interests them. You will be surprised at the odd things that are out of place which fascinate them. It should be an experience for them too.

TOP TIP: For a good day out with children, ask them what they want to do. A happy child is a pleasure and a lead to a stress-free adult.

Getting ready to go – survival gear

Getting around Venice is easy if you have all the right stuff and survival gear with you. You don't need much. Outlined below is a simple check list to save leaving everything to the last minute. It's the same travelling anywhere, simple things done beforehand can make your life easier, just as the just-in-timers tend to find out the hard way when it's all gone 'pete tong'.

Tin hats at the ready!

- Map. The ones in this book are good enough, but take a copy so you can put it in your pocket. It is much easier to do that then keep getting a book out. You can throw it away afterwards once it is well decimated and you have finished. Maps can also be found at the Tourist Information Office in Piazzale Roma. Get a good detailed one as Venice is like a maze and is quite complicated unless you have a very good sense of direction.
- Boat ticket. Get a vaporetto ticket for the day, as you will need it. It is the only way to cross the water, save getting wet, and your feet won't survive without it.
- Camera. Because you are going to be using it a lot, make sure you have spare charged batteries and plenty of space on the memory card.
- Bottle of water. Good idea, Sherlock. There may be shops, cafés and bars en route, but sometimes, depending on where you go or get

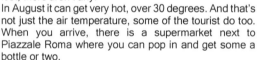

Don't take too much luggage

lost, there aren't any. In August it can get very hot, over 30 degrees. And that's not just the air temperature, some of the tourist do too. When you arrive, there is a supermarket next to Piazzale Roma where you can pop in and get some a bottle or two.

Good, but maybe not this good

- Shoes. You will need them, good ones which are easy to walk in as you are going to be using them a lot. There are some shoe shops in the city, but they tend to be very expensive and not the right type; better for going to the Ball rather than the walking the alleys.

- Book a tour. Only if you want to go with lots of other people and follow the red flag.
- Positive attitude. The most important thing next to the camera. Chill out and get in the mood, then the good times will roll. Remember, you are not on a mission, do less and see more to enjoy the whole experience.

Maybe not the gondola?

44

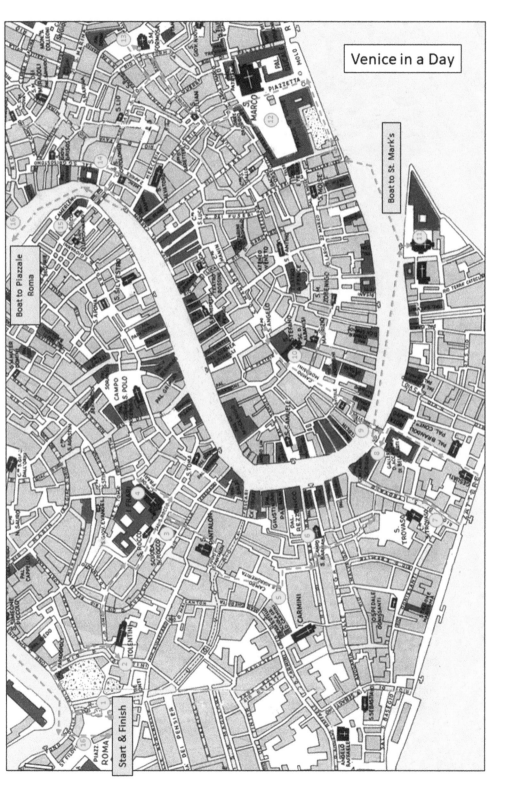

Venice in a Day

Boat to St. Mark's

Boat to Piazzale Roma

Start & Finish

Not a bad spot for lunch – The Grand Canal & the Salute from San Marco

Let's go - Venice in a day - What's en route.

This walk will take about half a day, excluding lengthy stops. Starting at Piazzale Roma, you can go either way, but I would suggest the way recommended. The itinerary below will show you round most of the main sights, including churches, museums and art galleries. En route, you will find many places of interest, plenty of wows to photograph and loads of cafés and bars to stop for some sustenance and a timeout.

The best way to walk the route is to follow the map carefully. If you get lost, go back to the last place and try again. The stops on the way are not far apart. Wherever you are, if you have time, just have a wander around the immediate area you are in. If you are after a gondola ride, there are sometimes one or two at the Frari, or try the Accademia Bridge or St Mark's, but the latter will be more crowded. Just keep your eyes open and negotiate. See 'Gondolas' in Chapter 2.

The pictures you see here are the views you will see on the walk and can help you visualise and navigate.

Start at Piazzale Roma – Scalzi Bridge

Get out when the sun goes down – San Marco & the Doge's Palace

1 Piazzale Roma. This is the starting and finishing point of the walk. Not the best place to be initiated in the glories of Venice, but it will only get better very soon. There is not much here except for lots of buses and people. But best to stop at the Tourist Information, get yourself a map, boat ticket for the vaporetto and supplies from the supermarket by the Grand Canal before you set off. When you are ready, head along the Grand Canal by the park and, just beyond it, over a bridge and turn immediate right along the smaller canal on your right. You will then be in the narrow canals, strolling past cafés and restaurants. Follow this canal and soon, you will find the Tolentini in a lovely square on your left.

2 Tolentini. (Full name: Chiesa di San Nicola da Tolentino). A small church built between 1591 and 1602, overlooking a piazza and the canal with attractive streets of cafés and restaurants in the immediate surrounding area. Lots of small hotels around here if you are looking for a convenient place to stay. Opening times. 8.30am-noon and 4.30pm-6.30pm Mon-Sat, and 4.30pm-6.30pm Sun.

From the church, head back along the canal to the right, then into Calle dei Amai, entering even narrower alleys - but persist, you will be lost soon. After crossing the bridge, turn right and follow round as it opens out into the piazza outside the Scuola Grande di San Rocco and the Frari.

3 Scuola Grande di San Rocco. The Scuola Grande di San Rocco is a lay confraternity founded in 1478. It is a unique site where over 60 paintings are preserved in their original setting in a building that has hardly undergone any alteration since its construction. See Chapter 2 for opening times and why it is a must visit.

The upstairs gallery

47

4   Frari. You will find this church opposite
the Scuola Grande di San Rocco. This is
one of the largest and one of the three
most important churches in Venice. An
imposing edifice, built of brick in the
Italian Gothic style, it was completed in
1338. Plain on the outside, but housing
many works of art on the inside, including
some major works by Titian. Opening
times. The church is open from 9am-6pm
Mon-Sat, and 1pm-6pm Sun, entry fee
€3.

Frari church

Round the side of the church at the front is a lovely piazza with a canal and a
few shops running along one side. One of the nicest in Venice I think, and a
good place to sit and watch the gondolas go by and have a siesta in the sun.

From here, go back towards the Scuola Grande di San Rocco and just before it
you will see a small entrance on the left in the shops with a sign to Accademia
and San Marco. Follow it over a bridge, take a right then an immediate left and
follow it to Campo San Pantalon. Go over the bridge on the opposite side of the
square and you will arrive in Campo Santa Margherita in a couple of minutes.

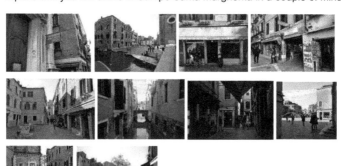

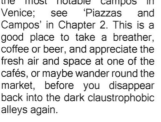

5   Campo Santa Margherita. One of
the most notable campos in
Venice; see 'Piazzas and
Campos' in Chapter 2. This is a
good place to take a breather,
coffee or beer, and appreciate the
fresh air and space at one of the
cafés, or maybe wander round the
market, before you disappear
back into the dark claustrophobic
alleys again.

Chilling out in the sunshine – Campo Margherita

From here head down the campo
following the fork to the left, then
a narrow street out of the campo round to the right into a wide street with
interesting shops and cafés. Go over the bridge at the end and follow the canal
left and you will arrive in Campo San Barnaba.

6   Campo San Barnaba. See Chapter 2, 'Piazzas and Campos'. This campo has one of the loveliest natural views in Venice. Amazing photos of the church and the campanile behind can be taken from many vantage points, and hopefully too some gondolas for added interest. Opening times. The church is open from 9.30am-7.30pm daily.

Campo San Barnaba

Go through the entrance on the far side of the campo signed Accademia and San Marco into Calle Lotto and follow it over two bridges. After the second one, turn right and in 5 minutes you will be at San Trovaso and the gondola workshops.

7   San Trovaso and gondola workshop. The Squero (boatyard) di San Trovaso is a small gondola boatyard that first opened in the 17th century. Back in the 16th century heyday of the gondola, there were upwards of 10,000 of these elegant boats plying the waters of Venice's canals. There are not too many here today - a mere 350.

Continue in the same direction to the Zattere where you will get a fantastic view of lagoon. Turn left. This is the waterfront where tall masted sailing ships used to moor up in days gone by, unloading all sorts of treasures and goods from distant lands. But now it is a good place for a stroll. It is worth stopping here for a

Gondola workshops – Dorsoduro

moment, or a bit longer for a cappuccino in a café, to take it all in and look at the view across to Giudecca and San Giorgio Maggiore. To continue, take the first left up beside the church, Rio Terra Foscarini, to the Accademia Galleries where the entrance is around the other side to the left.

8   Accademia Galleries. One of the top art galleries in Venice, which traces the development of Venetian art from the 14th to 18th centuries, with works by Bellini, Titian, Tintoretto, Veronese and Canaletto, amongst others. It includes Paolo Veronese's *Feast in the House of Levi*. Opening times. From 8.15am-2pm on Mondays and from 8.15am-7.15pm the rest of the week. There can be a long queue in the summer at busy periods, so it is advisable to get an advanced reservation to reserve your time by either calling the main number +39 041 520 0345 or via www.gallerieaccademia.org. Entry costs are €12 plus a €1.50 advanced reservation fee. If you are into art, this is one of the must do's, even if you visit no other gallery.

The Accademia Bridge is just next door.

9   Accademia Bridge. This bridge is one of the four main bridges over the Grand Canal; see Chapter 2. A good place to take photographs of classic views as the old masters saw them, especially the view of the Salute with its impressive and distinctive dome.

Choice of route. Depending on how well you are doing for time, and whether you are in need of a beer or an Aperol stop for a rest, there are two options here. For a detour,

View of the Salute from the Accademia Bridge

continue straight on over the bridge to Campo San Stefano where you will find many cafés and restaurants. Alternatively, or when you come back from Campo San Stefano, get the vaporetto No.1 a couple of stops straight to Santa Maria Salute on the same side of the Grand Canal. You can also walk there in about 10 minutes following the narrow alleys and squares, which are interesting too.

10   Campo San Stefano. Also described in 'Piazzas and Campos' in Chapter 2, you will find a very open square full of lots of cafés and shops. If you take the alley to the right just before the church, Calle dello Spezier, and then go to the end, cross then take a left at the far side of the square, you will see the leaning Santa Stefano Bell Tower and how it is propped up. Also, if you continue past the Santa Stefano church you will find the next campo, Campo Sant'Angelo, which is more rustic, with fewer shops or cafés. Here you will get the full perspective of the lean on the bell tower.

Coffee stop – Campo Santo Stefano

11   Santa Maria Salute. The third of the three most important churches in Venice along with the Basilica and the Frari. But it is the most represented church, both in paintings and photographs. This great Baroque church stands at the entrance to the Grand Canal. It was built in thanks to deliverance of the city from the plague and was completed in 1687. Inside it is quite sober, but has some works of art near the altar and on the ceiling. Opening times. From 9am-noon and 3pm-5.30pm, entrance fee €3 for adults.

Santa Maria Salute

From here take the vaporetto No.1 across the water to St Mark's Square.

12   Piazza San Marco. One of the most dramatic piazzas in Italy, but also full of tourists and, to some extent, it looks a bit shabby because of it. Hopefully you arrive here after 3pm where the queue for the Basilica and the Campanile should have died down; see Chapter 2. There are plenty of other things to look at here including the Doge's Palace, go up the Campanile or get a gold-plated coffee at one of the very expensive cafés which will leave little in your wallet or trash the limit on your credit card. But if that is your choice, try Café Florian, which may look stunning but has little atmosphere. Another couple of must sees, if you cannot miss

St Mark's from the Campanile

them, are the clock in the square (Torre dell'Orologio) and the views over the lagoon including the columns. You can also hire expensive gondolas rides here, but we aware that they queue up round the back of the Doge's Palace like the M25 on a Friday night. There are also some museums.

Opening times.

- Basilica - see Chapter 2.
- Doge's Palace or Palazzo Ducale, from 8.30am to 7pm in summer and 5.30 pm in winter, entrance fee €18 for adults, which includes Museo Correr.
- Campanile. From 9am-9pm in summer, 7.30pm in spring and autumn, and 9.30am-3.45pm in winter, entrance fee €8 for adults.

To get to the next stop, head out through the narrow alleyway under the clock, passing (hopefully!) a lot of expensive shops. At the end, turn right and go around the church ahead of you to the opposite side, down Campo de la Guerra and over the bridge at the end where you may find some interesting activity on the canal. Keep going straight in Calle Bande Castello which will take you over a bridge into the next amazing campo, Santa Maria Formosa.

Sunrise at St Mark's

13 Campo Santa Maria Formosa. This large square is flanked by some handsome palaces and, with its market, is one of the most charismatic in Venice. Next door is the Fondazione Querini Stampalia, which has a number of famous works of art. Opening times. From 10am-6pm (Tue-Sun), entrance fee €10 for adults.

Head out of the square in the same side you came in over the right-hand bridge by the church into Calle de Mondo Novo. Take a right on Salizada San Lio and follow straight on along Calle Sant'Antonio and over the bridge through the

Campo Santa Maria Formosa

arch into Sotoportego de la Bissa into Campo San Bartolomeo. There are plenty of shops en route, if you have not had enough of them already. This is the oldest part of Venice where the streets are really narrow, crowed and dark.

14   San Bartolomeo. A lively place with even more shops to be had as the alleys open out into the campo. This square is hidden away, but it is just next door to the Rialto Bridge. If you want to browse even more shops, follow to the opposite end of the square into Merceria, one of the premium shopping streets on the main drag which comes up from St Mark's Square.

To find the Rialto Bridge, take an exit along Salizzada Pio X, about half way along, and you will reach the bridge in one minute. Before you go up over the bridge, it is worth taking a left along Riva Ferro on the bank of the Grand Canal and taking in some of the views along there. A good place for a few photographs too. There are also a few restaurants if you are wanting to choose one with a view right on the Grand Canal.

Campo San Bartolomeo

15   Rialto Bridge and Markets. Follow up onto the Bridge in all its glories; see Chapter 2.

16   Back to Piazzale Roma. From the Bridge, take the No.1 vaporetto up the Grand Canal towards the station and Piazzale Roma. A recommendation is to do this at night, as it is a magical experience not to be missed. Stand at the back of the boat for the best view. At the end, you are back where you started, a day well spent with no annoying red flags or umbrellas and your head won't be spinning from information overload. You will sleep well, with the satisfaction of knowing that you have achieved it yourself, dreaming that you are drifting down the Grand Canal in a gondola watching all the magical buildings go by and a hunky gondolier at the back doing all the work.

The Grand Canal at night – Scalzi Bridge

Ponte degli Scalzi in the evening light

Chapter 5 - A Longer Visit

Exploring the neighbourhoods

Venice is built on a number of islands and the main city is made up of five key neighbourhoods divided by the Grand Canal. In addition to these five neighbourhoods, there are a large number of smaller islands in the Lagoon, some more famous and worth visiting than others.

Each neighbourhood tends to have its own characteristics, sense of community and architecture; some are more touristy, while others have a more local community feel. For a longer visit and to get a real perspective of the city, one should try to visit to all the five neighbourhoods and the islands of Murano, Giudecca and possibly Burano. The heart of the city is San Marco with the great Piazza, Basilica, and the Doge's Palace. Beyond these are a number of major attractions in the other neighbourhoods, such as the Accademia Galleries, the churches of the Frari and Salute, Ca' Rezzonico on the Grand Canal, then the quieter area of the Ghetto and the newer Arsenale.

Caffé Quadri Piazza – San Marco – expensive!

As far as cities go, Venice is very small and most of it can be visited on foot, if you have good feet. Additionally, between the various neighbourhoods, there is an efficient vaporetto service to help get about, and which also adds to the fun.

: beautiful colours of the buildings – San Polo

San Marco is the oldest part of the city, where the Doge set up his palace in the best place overlooking the Lagoon. It is the centre of many world-class attractions, and as a result is very popular; it includes the Piazza San Marco itself, the Basilica, the Campanile and the Doge's Palace. As it is very popular, this is where most of the tourists head. Because of its frontage onto the Grand Canal and the

San Polo, so many interesting alleys to explore and little boutiques

Lagoon, it also has most of the luxury hotels, restaurants and shops. But that is not all Venice is about. Make sure to also explore the back streets which are packed with galleries, boutiques, wine bars and a number of other imposing churches, which in addition to the Basilica are worth a visit.

San Polo and Santa Croce is where the Rialto Markets are, and what used to be the old red-light district and the centre of business and commerce in centuries gone by. But behind the façade of the Grand Canal are narrow backstreets full of small restaurants, local bars and interesting shops. The central attraction is the church of Frari and the Scuola di San Rocco next door. Even so, it is a less touristy and a more relaxing part of the city to explore.

Dorsoduro is on the opposite side of the Grand Canal from San Marco. It is home to two world-class galleries, the Accademia and the Peggy Guggenheim Collection. It is a quiet pretty neighbourhood with shaded squares, quiet canals and picturesque residences belonging to wealthy Venetians. The Zattere provides an amazing place for a stroll, overlooking the Lagoon and the neighbouring island of Giudecca.

Cannaregio is where the locals live

The quiet streets of the Castello

Cannaregio is on northern side of the Grand Canal. Just a couple of streets beyond the Strada Nova, the streets are deserted. Three canals run the length of the neighbourhood with the Ghetto and the Jewish community at the centre. This is one of the most local of the neighbourhoods with over one third of the city's population living here. This is a place to stop off at those remote coffee shops and watch the local people and the world go by.

Castello is at the eastern end of the city. Again, it is a quieter area than San Marco with no teeming hordes. Some luxury hotels sprawl along the front of the Lagoon, but otherwise quiet squares and fine remote churches populate the back alleys. At the far end are the imposing gates of the Arsenale. The main attraction is the Riva degli Schiavoni, the long promenade running along the Lagoon up to San Marco.

View from the Rialto Bridge at night

The Islands make up much of the Lagoon. The best ones to visit are Murano for its glassworks, Burano for its beauty, and Giudecca for the view across the Lagoon to the main city. The Lido is good for the beach, but not much else as it is populated by modern hotels and cars.

Planning a longer visit

The optimum time for a visit to Venice is about 4 days and 3 nights. This will give you time to see the best of the city without rushing around. It's all about taking your time, and not trying to do it all in the first 24 hours. To make the most of it, it is well worth planning in advance the sort of things you want to do. There are plenty of options:

- See the historic buildings, squares and streets while stopping off in coffee shops to take in the view and atmosphere, and also giving your feet a rest, because they are going to take some punishment.
- Spend time taking photographs or selfies which include many world-renowned historic sights and vistas. How many 'look at me' pictures are there of Venice on Facebook? People love it. With a little patience you can also take some amazing photos, certainly of

Little restaurants in the back streets are the best – San Polo

the architecture but also the light can make some amazing compositions, like some of those I hope you appreciate in this book. Maybe early one morning see the sunrise over the Lagoon at St Mark's Square or take the Grand Canal in the evening at twilight. Just some ideas.
- Visit museums and galleries to understand the history of the city. Even if you are not into these, you will be awed by some of the best in dramatic settings.
- Go shopping. Once you have sifted through the tourist junk, there are some amazing things to buy. Wine, genuine Murano glass, Italian shoes and posh clothes from boutiques.
- Theatres. There are three theatres in the city, La Fenice being the most famous.
- Markets. Get up early one morning and see the Rialto Markets in action and buy some fresh produce for dinner.
- Events. There are events and regattas all through the year; check the websites for what is going on.
- Sample the local cuisine. Stop off for lunch, or find a nice romantic restaurant for dinner.
- Go for a ride in a gondola, there is nowhere else in the world where you can do this (Las Vegas does not count, as they are fake).
- Or just walk and wander, this is what Venice is all about.

Surprises around every corner – Cannaregio

When planning, consider everyone's aspirations and what they want to do. Plan an itinerary for a pace and places which suit the group you are with. Allow for time to look at things and visit attractions. You will not have time to do everything. Also to make things more interesting, plan for something different every day.

The walks in the following chapters allow you to cover each of the neighbourhoods and

see the main sights in each one. Each one can be covered in about half a day, but you may want to spend longer looking at things. The good thing is that you will see something different on each walk without repeating where you have just been.

Everything is worth looking at

TOP TIP: Good planning will enable you to spend more time enjoying the city rather than trying to figure it out when you get there. More fun with less stress.

TOP TIP: Regardless of planning, you should still go with the unexpected, that's what the real Venice is all about. Surprises around every corner.

Everyone goes by boat

Example itinerary for 4 days

Most people consider going to Venice for a long weekend, setting out on a Thursday , arriving mid to late morning, and going back home Sunday evening. The itinerary below gives some ideas for a 4-day visit to Venice.

Day 1 - The purpose of the day is to gently get into seeing the city after a long flight or train journey to Venice. Take it easy over the first afternoon, but feel like you have seen something without getting caught up in large crowds. A wander through the Dorsoduro to St Mark's Square seeing some of the main sights is an ideal way to get into the

Idyllic – Cannaregio

atmosphere of the city and relax with a stop for a late lunch.

- Arrive in Venice mid to late morning and check into your hotel and leave your baggage; you won't want it after climbing the stairs over the first few bridges.
- If not already purchased at the airport - get a 3-day vaporetto ticket from the kiosk in Piazzale Roma.
- Set off from Piazzale Roma following the start of the walk to see Venice in a day in Chapter 4. It is best to leave an in-depth visit of the major sights, like the Frari and San Rocco, for another day when you have more time to take them in and are less tired from travelling (the choice is yours).

Gondolas waiting for a ride at the Rialto

- Stop for a drink and a sandwich in Campo Santa Margherita to refresh and have some lunch. Aperol spritzers (that orange drink) are favourite on a hot day.
- Take in the views from the Accademia Bridge.
- Either take the vaporetto No.1 direct to St Mark's Square or wander down to the Salute and take the vaporetto to St Mark's Square from there.
- Getting to St Mark's Square mid to late afternoon is good. If the queue is short, it's a good idea to see one or two of the sights, either the Basilica or a trip up the Campanile.
- After this, it is time to get off your feet, have a drink at L'Ombra del Leone, just along the Grand Canal from Harry's bar and much cheaper, with a terrace overlooking the Salute and the Grand Canal. The terrace in the Hotel Bauer Palazzo next door is not bad either.

- Having had an early start, time to consider an early dinner. Take the boat back to your hotel and find a local restaurant nearby.
- After dinner, if you still have the energy, take the boat back to St Mark's and see it at night, with a romantic trip back up the Grand Canal to see out the evening. If you are lucky, you will see the moon glinting over the Lagoon.

Day 2 - A day to see some of the other neighbourhoods.

- If you fancy a really early start, head down to St Mark's and see the sunrise over the Lagoon and then get some well earnt pre-breakfast croissants at one of the cafés at the Rialto Bridge. Afterwards see the Rialto Markets as they set up for the day.
- Head back to your hotel for breakfast.
- After breakfast, head out on the Cannaregio walk (Chapter 8), seeing

Canal-side restaurants – Santa Croce

the quieter areas of the Ghetto and the church of Santi Giovanni e Paolo, finishing at the Rialto Bridge, maybe a good place to have some lunch.

Quiet tranquil backwaters – Santa Croce

- After lunch, follow the walk around San Polo and Santa Croce (Chapter 7), either joining the circuit at the Rialto Bridge or going back to Piazzale Roma and following from there. Here you can do a bit more relaxation and little shopping.
- En route you will see the Frari, the Scuola di San Rocco and the large Campo San Polo.
- Between the Rialto Bridge and the Campo San Polo, you will find many alleyways full of interesting shops.
- Remember to stop for a coffee en route at one of the squares; it's all about watching the people and taking in the local atmosphere.
- Towards the end of the afternoon, it may be a good time to go on a boat trip, and make some use of the vaporetto ticket before you head back to your hotel to get ready to go out for dinner.
- For dinner, choose a nice restaurant somewhere special. There are plenty to choose from depending on whether your taste is expensive, rustic or a particular local Venetian cuisine; see 'Restaurants' in Chapter 10.

Just finished up the local cuisine – Campo San Margherita

Day 3 - This is a day to experience and spend more time seeing the sights you particular want visit in Venice. More of a day to relax.

- After breakfast, start with a trip to Murano to see some glassworks and one of the more attractive islands. Walk along the central canal to the far end and get the vaporetto from one of the stops on the far side back to the main city.
- On return, you may want to take a gondola ride. A good place is the gondola station near the Ca' d'Oro vaporetto stop.
- After this amazing experience you will always remember, take the vaporetto to the Accademia Bridge, maybe see the Accademia Galleries or the Peggy Guggenheim Collection and then follow the walk for San Marco and Castello (Chapter 6) in the afternoon.
- You will see the amazing squares of San Stefano, La Fenice (the main theatre), the Bovolo, to the shopping area in Campo San Bartolomeo.
- The walk will enable you to experience the narrow streets to the amazing square at Campo Santa Maria Formosa.

- Then head off through the quieter area of Castello via a couple of important churches, Santi Giovanni e Paolo and San Francesco della Vigna, to the Arsenale.
- From there you can stroll up the Riva degli Schiavoni back to St Mark's Square.
- You may choose to go to the theatre tonight or find somewhere different for dinner.

Locals hard at work – loads of atmosphere

Day 4 - This is a day to experience some of the places you would like to go back to or one of the sights you want to take a little more time over.

Whatever you do, one option, if you are still fit and not had enough, is to do the walk around the Dorsoduro and Giudecca, ending up in the Campo San Margherita or near the Rialto Bridge and find a nice restaurant for a late lunch to end the trip before heading for the airport or the train station to make your way home.

There you have it, a very busy 4 days, but you will have achieved a lot, had a great time, with an immense sense of inner fulfilment that you have seen some of the best Venice has to offer. A lifetime of memories you can talk to your friends about for hours. I am sure it will be on Facebook already before you get home!

All this without feeling you have been marauded by vast crowds of unruly tourists. If you want to go slow, it may be worth considering splitting the itinerary into two visits. That works too.

Campo Barnaba – Dorsoduro

St Mark's at its best, early in the morning sunrise 6.30 am

The Grand Canal at its best, early evening sunset at the Rialto Bridge

Chapter 6 - Getting Out and About - San Marco & Castello

San Marco & Castello - the area

San Marco is the oldest part of the city. This is where the Doge set up his palace overlooking the Lagoon, while Castello at the eastern end of the city, which is next door, is much newer. San Marco is the centre of many world-class sights and as a result is very popular, including the main square itself, the Basilica, the Campanile and the Doge's Palace. This is the area where most of the tourists head and to many, St Mark's Square is Venice done, so they miss out on much more. As well as the major sights around St Mark's Square, there are numerous sights to see, especially around the back streets including other attractive churches and squares which would be a major sight elsewhere if they were on their own.

St Mark's Square

TOP TIP: San Marco is a must-see area but be sure to explore the back alleys and surrounding area too.

The walk

This walk will take you on a trip around the whole area, showing you some of the best parts. The experience will include taking you down the back alleys where you will feel totally lost and see some of the other beautiful squares and churches. It will take about 3 hours plus stopping off time. Some of the darkest, narrowest and scariest alleys are in this part of the city where it can get really claustrophobic, especially at night.

The walk starts at the Accademia Bridge, where from the top there is a wonderful view of the Salute down the Grand Canal. Heading north over the bridge into Campo Santo Stefano, which exudes life and energy around its cafés and the church. Here you will get a feel of real Venice. Following through to the next square, Campo Sant'Angelo is a much quieter place with just a couple of cafés and a more residential feel; it still has atmosphere, but is different. Here you can see the lean on the tower of the church of Santo Stefano.

Early morning sunrise – look no tourists!

Then follow the narrow alleys through to the Teatro la Fenice, Venice's premium theatre. If you can, it's worth getting a visit to see the splendour of the theatre inside; see Chapter 2 for what it looks like. More tiny alleys will take you to the Scala Contarini del Bovolo, tucked away in this hard-to-find place, but what a find.

From here we head to the church of San Salvatore and the shopping area around Campo San Bartolomeo and the Rialto Bridge. This is one of the best places to take photographs of the Grand Canal. Once you have taken your pictures, we follow narrow streets of shops until they open up into Campo Santa Maria Formosa. In this amazing square you will find the church and the palace Fondazione Querini Stampalia, which is worth a visit to see the library with its major works of art.

Palazzo Contarini dei Bovolo

Horses of St Mark's

The next stop is heading into Castello where there are two major churches, Santi Giovanni e Paolo and Francesco della Vigna. From here the tourists really do thin out until you reach the Arsenale, which was one of the largest naval dock yards in the world.

St. Mark's – Just as beautiful at night

Follow the canal to the Riva degli Schiavoni, which is the promenade that runs alongside the Lagoon, and wander past a number of imposing top-end hotels back to St Mark's Square. The key sights to see include the church at San Zaccaria, inside the ultra-posh Hotel Danieli, and the Bridge of Sighs. The Danieli is where you can dream of where you might have been staying at over €1000 a night, rather than the Doge's prison next door.

A few more metres along the Riva degli Schiavoni, you are at the finish at St Mark's Square with all its major sights.

At the end of all this, you should find a bar for a well-earnt beer or two. One suggestion is L'Ombra del Leone, which has a terrace overlooking the Grand Canal and the Salute, just along from St Mark's.

TOP TIP: If it looks like there is going to be a good sunset, the Giardini vaporetto stop at the eastern end of Castello is a good place to view it from.

L'Ombra del Lenoi

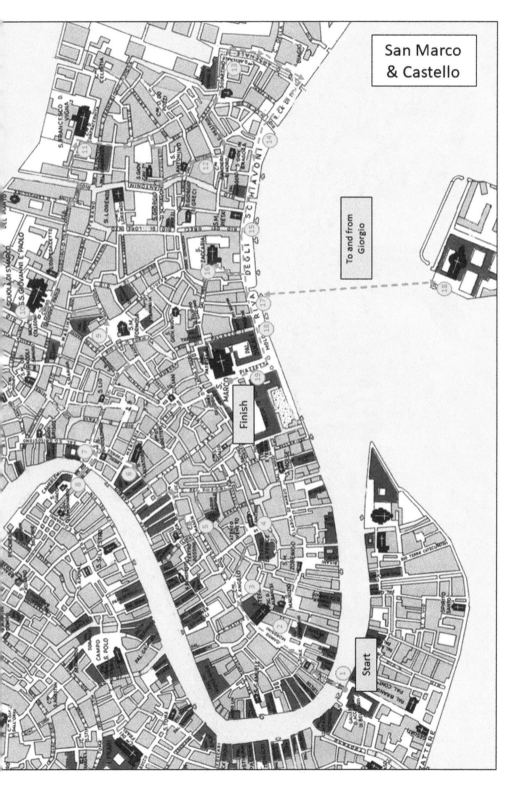

San Marco
& Castello

To and from
Giorgio

Finish

Start

What's en route?

To start the walk, head for the Accademia Bridge. This walk will take about 3 hours plus time for looking at things. The best way to get around is to follow the map carefully. If you get lost, go back to the last place and try again. Wherever you are, if you have time, just have a wander around the immediate area you are in. To help you visualise and navigate, the small pictures below are the views you will see on the walk.

Ponte dell'Accademia

1   Accademia Bridge. This bridge is one of the four main bridges over the Grand Canal; see Chapter 2. Before you set off, this is a good place to take some photographs, especially of the classic views of the Grand Canal as the old masters saw them centuries ago. From the Bridge, head straight on to Campo Santo Stefano.

2   Campo Santo Stefano. Also described in 'Piazzas and Campos' in Chapter 2, you will find a very open square full of lots of cafés, a good place for a coffee and one of those sticky Venetian pastries. If you take the alley to the right just before the church, Calle dello Spezier, and go to the end, then take a left at the far side of the square, you will see the leaning Santo Stefano Bell Tower and the buttress propping it up. These towers do fall down. The Campanile in St Mark's Square fell down many years ago and was rebuilt.

Campo Santo Stefano

To continue, return to the square and head on past the church, and keep going straight down Calle dei Frati, going over a bridge into the next campo (Campo Sant'Angelo), which is quieter with a few shops and cafés. It has a residential atmosphere with locals going about their business.

3   Campo Sant'Angelo. From here you will get a different perspective of the lean on the bell tower of the church of Santo Stefano as if it is going to topple like a Jenga. A good place to take a photograph. Also, you will notice large stone enclosures in the middle of the square. They have a purpose. These are wells where the locals used to get their water. You will see them in most squares around Venice. Now you won't forget. Drinking fountains have some of the best water in Venice.

To continue, take the right-hand narrow alley in the corner and follow over a canal to Campiello Fenice. Follow left round the theatre to the square at the front.

4   Teatro la Fenice is the city's oldest theatre, built in 1792. A fire destroyed it in 1996, but it was restored by 2003. There are regular operas and concerts and it is possible to make a visit during the day for €9, but only if you book in advance. See Chapter 2.

Leave the theatre by the Calle del Frutarol, over a bridge and take the next alley to the left into Calle Fuseri. This is where the alleys get even narrower and the Bovolo can be a bit of a challenge to find. Over another canal and take the second left into an even narrower alley, Calle Locande. The Bovolo is signed just down this small alley on the left.

Inside the theatre

5   Scala Contarini del Bovolo. This palazzo is best known for its graceful external staircase. It is not possible to go in, but it makes a spectacular picture - and well done for finding it.

From the Bovolo, turn left and follow the alley round the right into Campo Manin with a statue in the centre. There are some modern buildings here which are not so nice. Follow the right-hand side of a large grey one and round to the left to Calle de St Luca. Take the Corte Teatro on the left and turn right into Calle del Teatro,

Bovolo Palace

straight on into Calle del Lovo, over a bridge until you arrive at the front of Chiesa di San Salvador on the right-hand side.

6   San Salvatore. The interior of the church is a fine example of Venetian Renaissance architecture and well worth a visit. The current church is as designed by Giorgio Spavento in the early 16th century. Opening times. 9am-noon and 4pm-6.30pm Mon-Sat, entrance fee, free.

San Salvatore church

To find Campo San Bartolomeo, turn right out of the church and you will find it teeming with shops and people just about 100 metres up.

7   San Bartolomeo. A lively place with even more shops than San Marco as the alley opens out into the Campo. This square is hidden away, but it is just next door to the Rialto Bridge. As well as the expensive shops in the square, there are many more interesting boutiques after your credit card in the adjoining alleyways.

To find the Rialto Bridge, take the exit in the middle of the square up Salizzada Pio X and you will reach the bridge in one minute. Before you go up over the bridge, it is worth taking a left along Riva Ferro, by the bank of the Grand Canal, and taking in some of the views along there. There are also a few restaurants if you are wanting to choose one with a view and seat right on the Grand Canal. It can be very busy with a lot going on around here, but even better if you get a good seat to watch it all.

Lively Campo San Bartolomeo

8 Rialto Bridge and Markets. See Chapter 2. The markets are part of the San Polo walk; see Chapter 7. But you can extend this one to include them. They are well worth exploring.

From the bridge continue back to Campo San Bartolomeo and take the small alley to the right at the north end of the square just beyond the statue, Sotoportego de la Bissa. Follow the shops over a canal into Calle Sant'Antonio, bearing round to the right into

Rialto Markets

Salizada San Lio. Near the end, take a left turn into Calle del Mondo Novo or the next one, Calle Bande Castello, both of which will take you to Campo Santa Maria Formosa.

9 Campo Santa Maria Formosa. This large square is flanked by some handsome palaces and, with its market, it is one of the most charismatic in Venice. Next door is the Fondazione Querini Stampalia which has a number of famous works of art and is one of the best preserved house museums in Venice.

Campo Santa Maria Formosa

TOP TIP: This is one of the most photogenic squares for taking natural pictures of Venice's architecture and local life going on.

Head out of the square on the opposite side into Calle Lunga Santa Maria Formosa. At about the third alley on the left, turn left into a very narrow alley, Calle Cicogna Castello, over a bridge into Calle Bressana to reach the church at Santi Giovanni e Paolo, such an amazing view as you pop out of the dark narrow passage, which looks like a hole in the side of the building, into the Campo.

Activity in the backwaters

10   Santi Giovanni e Paolo. This church is situated in a wonderful square, well worth having a break to sit in the sunshine and take it all in. Next door is the Scuola Grande di San Marco, a hospital originally built as one of the six great confraternities in the city. In the centre is the statue of a horse, Bartolomeo Colleoni. Opening times. 9am-6pm Mon-Sat and noon-6pm Sun, entrance fee, €2.50 for adults.

Santi Giovanni e Paolo

Leave the square by the side of the church, heading down Barbaria de le Tole. From here the tourists almost disappear. At the end take a right and then a left over a bridge. After the bridge, turn left and take the first right into San Francesco della Vigna down the street of the same name as the church.

11   San Francesco della Vigna. The church was built in the 13th century and is a purer and simpler affair compared with some of the others, but it is still a big church and, if you have not had enough of them, well worth a visit. The inside has a rich collection of works of art including paintings and sculptures. Opening times. 8am-12.30pm and 3pm-7pm, entrance fee, €3 for adults

San Francesco della Vigna

Pigeons everywhere

From the church, head left from the main door, going under some pillars and over a canal. Go to the end and take a left and a right along Salizada de le Gatte. You will pass a big mural on the wall. Take a turn to the right through Campiello de la Gatte, and then left and right into Calle Furlani to the bridge at the end. Now you are really in the maze, with very few people about. Turn left along the canal just before the bridge and go down to the next bridge, turning left into Salizada Sant'Antonin. Follow round to the right and turn right into the big square at the end with the church of Chiesa di San Giovanni Battista in Bragora.

71

12   Chiesa di San Giovanni Battista in Bragora. This is a simple church built in the 1400s. The square will give you a bit of breathing space from the narrow streets, with a café and somewhere to sit down, but it may be better to wait until the next stop at the Arsenale for a proper coffee.

From the square, take the next left from where you entered the square into Calle Crosera. Take a left into the narrow alley, Calle del Pestrin, on the

Chiesa di San Giovanni Battista in Bragora

corner and follow to the end, round to the right over the bridge. Go straight on past the church, keeping the canal on the left until you arrive at the imposing gates of the Arsenale.

13   Arsenale. The Arsenale is a more recent addition to Venice. This is a good place to stop and take in the view from one of the cafés, stopping for a coffee or a beer, maybe a sandwich if you have missed lunch. The Arsenale is the centre of the city's maritime heritage and was at one time the greatest shipyard in the world. At its peak, 16,000 Venetians were employed to build, equip and repair the great Venetian galleys (ropey old wooden boats to you and me). Behind the gates, it is like a city within a city, with its own workshops, warehouses, factories, foundries and docks, but little access to the public.

Gates of the Arsenale – Good place for a snack

To get to the Riva degli Schiavoni, just cross the bridge and follow the canal to the right down to the Lagoon.

Amazing views from the Campanile of St Mark's – Riva degli Schiavoni

Riva degli Schiavoni

14   Riva degli Schiavoni. See Chapter 2. The promenade can become very crowded, so a bit of patience may be required. But on the plus side you will get beautiful views of the Lagoon including the church tower and island of San Giorgio Maggiore.

San Giorgio dei Creci

15   San Giorgio dei Creci. On the way along the Riva degli Schiavoni, after passing the Metropole Hotel, a view of the leaning bell tower of San Giorgio dei Creci can be seen from the bridge. Another one that may bite the dust soon.

16   San Zaccaria. Next to the Savoia & Jolanda hotel is a narrow passage way to San Zaccaria. Follow this for about 100 metres and you will reach a quiet square with the church of the same name. This can be a welcome relief from the hubbub of the promenade outside. The square backs onto alleys of shops which are the overspill from St Mark's Square. The alleys and canals around here are worth a little exploring with attractive little canal side cafés and boutiques, and canals usually filled with gondolas going by. Opening times. 10am-noon and 4pm-6pm Mon-Sat and 4pm-6pm Sun, entrance fee, free.

San Zaccaria

17   Hotel Danieli. Head back out onto the Riva degli Schiavoni. Two doors down is the Hotel Danieli. Don't be put off by the attentive nature of the doormen. Just politely walk straight in as if you are staying there. It is worth a visit inside just for the wow factor of one of Venice's premium hotels. You will be amazed. This is wow at its best.

Continue 50 metres, and the Bridge of Sighs can be found on the right.

Hotel Danieli

Bridge of Sighs – Gondola jam!

18   Bridge of Sighs. The bridge was built in about 1600, for the purpose of connecting the Doge's Palace with the new prisons. It takes its name from the sighs of the prisoners crossing on their last trip of life to their final destiny with feelings of despair.

If you want to go to the church of San Giorgio Maggiore, take a No.2 or N vaporetto here from the San Marco Zaccaria vaporetto station to nip across the water; it takes about 5 to 10 minutes.

Continue along the Riva degli Schiavoni, and Piazza San Marco can be found 50 metres along on the right.

19   Piazza San Marco. One of the most dramatic piazzas in Italy, but also full of tourists and to some extent a bit shabby because of it. Hopefully arrive here after 3pm and the queue for the Basilica will have died down; see Chapter 2. There are plenty of other things to do here including the Doge's Palace, go up the

Piazza San Marco

The Florian coffee shop – lots of €€€

Campanile or chill out in some very expensive cafés or bar in the main square which will leave you a little short of change on your bank card. There are also a couple of museums: Museo Correr with its picture galleries of old masters, and Museo Archeologico, full of sculptures produced by Venetian artists. Finally, the Zecca on the Lagoon front near the columns used to be the city's mint. This is where all the real money was made.

TOP TIP: If the queue is short, don't miss the opportunity to go up to the top of the Campanile, the view of Venice is amazing.

There you have it, a trip around some of the best sights in the world, done in half a day. Time for a drink. A suggested bar is L'Ombra del Leone, which has a terrace overlooking the Grand Canal and the Salute; see location and above map. It is much cheaper than most of the alternatives, but you have to put up with the pigeons. They are not too bad really. But you do get a good beer and plenty of nibbles and a stick to fend them off.

Friendly bird

Pigeon whacker supplied

Beautiful reflections

Chapter 7 - Getting Out and About - Santa Croce & San Polo

Santa Croce & San Polo - the area

Santa Croce and San Polo are two adjacent neighbourhoods on the southern side of the Grand Canal. Once you get away from Piazzale Roma and the bus station into the old city, it gets much better. These neighbourhoods are much quieter and more relaxing to explore than San Marco, and this is also where the red-light district used to be, with the ladies doing their trade down the seedy dark alleys. Both areas were named after churches which stood within their boundaries. The first communities became established in the 11th century and grew to become the commercial hub of Venice.

Little canals, boutique hotels and restaurants – Santa Croce

Around the Rialto Markets and Bridge, San Polo is still one of the liveliest sestieri of the city; it has a less touristy feel than San Marco, with many small shops, market stalls, restaurants and local bars to enjoy.

The area around the bustle of the market gives way to a maze of alleyways full of small interesting shops, opening up into the campo of San Polo. The other main attractions are the Frari and the Scuola Grande di San Rocco in Santa Croce.

The walk

This walk will take you on a trip, showing you the best of the neighbourhood - except for Piazzale Roma, where you start. It

Interesting alleyways – San Polo

will take about 3 hours. You will see amazing churches and squares while getting lost down the back alleys and experiencing the Rialto Markets.

Starting at Piazzale Roma, follow the Grand Canal into the city where there are wonderful views from the Scalzi Bridge before heading into the narrow alleyways. In a short time, the alleyways will open up into the campo of San Giacomo dell'Orio, which with its cafés, restaurants and church will offer an amazing perspective of what Venice is all about. From here we follow a rabbit

Canal side restaurants – Santa Croce

warren of small alleys, passing picturesque canal side views with gondolas, and quaintly tucked-away restaurants, before arriving at the Rialto food markets. Continuing through the tourist markets, we soon arrive at the Rialto Bridge, a masterpiece of Venice architecture, where you can stop and take in this amazing monument to the past and admire the views down the Grand Canal.

The scene changes as we walk past the restaurants and cafés

Early morning light – Santa Croce

Rialto markets opening up – San Polo

on the edge of the Grand Canal before heading into small alleyways full of interesting shops. A good area to explore. From the shops, the alleys open out into the large campo of San Polo; see 'Piazzas and campos' in Chapter 2. A few more alleys further lead to the stunning square at the front of the Frari, with its canal side setting and local shops. The Frari, and the Scuola Grande di San Rocco behind it, are two of the major sights one should see.

There is a short extension of the walk to the Campo San Pantalon and its church before heading back via the Tolentino and picture-perfect canals and cafés to finish back in Piazzale Roma, possibly stopping in one of these little establishments for a coffee.

What's en route?

To start the walk, head for the Piazzale Roma. The best way to get around is to follow the map carefully. If you get lost, go back to the last place and try again. Wherever you are, if you have time, just have a wander around the immediate area you are in. To help you visualise and navigate, the small pictures below are the views you will see on the walk.

Plenty of little restaurants – Santa Croce

Santa Croce
& San Polo

GLI SCALZI

Start & Finish

PIAZZ.
ROMA

1 Piazzale Roma. This is the starting and finishing point. Not the best place to be initiated in the beauty of Venice, but it will only get better from here. There is not much here except a lot of buses and people. If you do not already have them, best to stop off at the Tourist Information to get yourself a map and a boat pass for the vaporetto, and make sure to get supplies from the supermarket by the Grand Canal before you set off.

Grand Canal and Scalzi Bridge

When you are ready, head off along the Grand Canal to the right. Keeping the Grand Canal on your left, go over a stone bridge, past the park and over a second bridge. As you walk along the promenade past a few shops, cafés and hotels, you will see the Scalzi Bridge ahead. On the opposite side of the Grand Canal is the main station where some famous trains like the Orient Express arrive. Alternatively, going over the new Costituzione Bridge and up the far side of the Grand Canal to the Scalzi Bridge is a better place to take pictures of the busy canal scene of boats going up and down, as you will get the old buildings in the background and not the station. Either choice is good.

2 Scalzi Bridge. The Scalzi Bridge is one of four major crossing points along the Grand Canal. Most tourists from Piazzale Roma now head over the new Costituzione Bridge and join the rest of the hordes from the station on the far side. The top of the Scalzi Bridge is an excellent place to take a photograph or two, giving the long perspective of the Grand Canal and the amazing architecture on both sides.

Evening view from the Scalzi Bridge

From the top of the bridge, take the narrow alley straight ahead, Calle Lunga, away from the Grand Canal. Take the second left, going over a bridge, and turn right immediately alongside the canal, going down Fondamenta Garzotti, which is an attractive canal. Follow down to a triangular square at the second bridge (a contradiction I know, but it works). Take the tiny alley in the corner and follow through, taking a left and immediate right into the next square. Go past the well, and as the square narrows, take the tiny archway on

The big people at the Rialto Markets

the left just before house no.1045. Go through into the next courtyard. Take the archway on the far right-hand side, over a bridge and follow into Campo San Giacomo dell'Orio.

3   Church and Campo San Giacomo dell'Orio. This an attractive square with a number of interesting shops, cafés and restaurants where you can sit out in the sunshine. One or two of the restaurants around here up to La Zucca at the next stop are rated quite highly on TripAdvisor. The Romanesque church of San Giacomo forms the focal point and can provide a cool sanctuary on a hot day. It was rebuilt in 1225 and has a number of artworks within. Opening times. The church is open 10am-5pm Mon-Sat, entrance fee €3 for adults.

Church of San Giacomo dell'Orio

It is worth having a wander round the square and looking at the views from the bridges behind the church. To continue, exit through the trees in the north-east corner into Calle Larga Rossa.

4   Calle Larga Rossa restaurants and Canal. This is an interesting and quite attractive street of small shops with a lovely offset bridge at the end and restaurants on both sides. It is nice place to sit out for a coffee or a spot of lunch and watch the gondolas regularly going by.

Go over the bridge past La Zucca (a vegetarian restaurant), then round to the left at the end and take the next alley immediately on the right, over a bridge to the end.

Calle Larga Rossa

You will find most of the turns around this maze of alleys are signposted to the Rialto in the direction you are going and Ferrovia Roma the other way. You will

81

find a lot of little shops along here. At the end, turn left and the Museo di Palazzo Mocenigo is just on the right past the sign for the Rialto.

5   Museo di Palazzo Mocenigo. This is a dazzling 17th century waterside palace, which was part of the Venice aristocracy and was owned by Count Alvise Nicolo Mocenigo. As well as the architecture and furniture in the beautiful rooms upstairs, there is a collection of historic fashion belonging to the duchess and an exhibition dedicated to fragrance, from when

Museo di Palazzo Mocenigo

Venice was Europe's capital of perfume. Opening times. The palazzo is open from 10am-4pm Tue-Sun, entrance fee €8 for adults.

To get to the next stop, turn right out of the museum and walk up to the Grand Canal where you will find the church of San Stae on the waterfront.

6   Church of San Stae. The church sits in a small attractive isolated square overlooking the Grand Canal. It was built in 1709 and restored in 1977. It contains some works of art by Tiepolo and Piazzetta and was one of the churches Turner painted in the morning light over the Grand Canal. Opening times. The church is open from 1.45pm-4.30pm Mon-Sat, entrance fee €3 for adults.

Church of San Stae

To find the Ca' Pesaro Galleria, turn right out of the church, over the bridge and take the first left down a narrow alley at the end of the covered way. The gallery is just over the bridge at the end.

7   Ca' Pesaro Galleria. The gallery used to be a palace owned by the Pesaro family. It is full of many treasures, as it is now a gallery for major Italian artists of the 19th and 20th centuries and also has a collection of Chinese and Indian artefacts. Opening times. The gallery is open from 10am-5pm (6pm in summer) Tue-Sun, entrance fee €14 for adults.

Ca' Pesaro

From here it is a maze of alleys to the Rialto Markets. On leaving the Ca'Pesaro, follow the canal and take the first left at the bridge into Calle dei Ravano. Go over a bridge and at the end turn right into Calle Corner. Take the second left into Calle dei Morti. Go over the bridge and follow round to the right down the steps into Campo Cassiano.

Exit the square alongside the church. You can follow the signs to the Rialto, zigzagging through the back alleys. Go left at the next and then follow the sign right after about 30 metres. Then go through a narrow set of archways going over a bridge into Calle de le Do Spade, turning left at the end and second right into Calle Galiazza. You will then be at the Rialto Markets.

Alternatively for a nice view of the Grand Canal, from Campo Cassiano, turn left round the church at the end of the square into Calle del Campaniel to the Grand Canal. Turn right and follow the canal promenade to the Rialto Markets.

8   Rialto Bridge and Markets. See Chapter 2.
The first market you will find is the fish   Rialto fish market early morning
market. It is worth spending some time
here wandering around all the markets before you head to the Rialto Bridge. Here you will find the fresh fish which will be on your restaurant table at dinner time. But remember, it is best to get here early as all the action tends to be all over by lunch time. It is a good place to take some interesting photographs of some of the weird and wonderful creatures fished from the Lagoon and of the market scenes with the Grand Canal in the background.

9   Riva del Vin. The Riva del Vin is a promenade that runs along the Grand Canal from the Rialto Bridge to the church of San Silvestro, on the San Polo side. It is full of cafés, bars and restaurants, many of which have seating alongside the Grand Canal. This is one of the few stretches of the Grand Canal actually flanked by pavements. It gets its name from the time when boats laden with wine would land here and moor up to unload. The setting is perfect for both lunch and dinner with plenty of atmosphere and activity. The only drawback is the prices, which can be much higher, with lower

Riva del Vin

quality. Check reviews and recommendations before deciding. If eating in a restaurant is too expensive, then this is also a good place to sit down on the waterside and eat your own fresh sandwich purchased earlier. What a good idea. It is quite an interesting place to stop for a while and chill out.

After taking some stunning photographs of the Rialto Bridge, to get to the next port of call, continue down the promenade to where it widens out just before the end, and turn right into Rio Terra S. Silvestro. Take the next left and then a right, still in Rio Terra S. Silvestro.

You will see more shops and quieter restaurants. Take the next left, signposted to Piazzale Roma, into Calle de L'ogio o de la Rugheta. You are now in a narrower alley of even more interesting shops. It is well worth having a browse around the streets here.

View from the Rialto Bridge

Follow to the end into a small campo, Campo Sant'Aponal, taking the centre alley on the far side, signposted Piazzale Roma. At the end, turn right, then immediately left through a small attractive square at the end of two opposite canals into Calle dei Meloni. Follow to the end, over a bridge into Campo San Polo.

10   Campo San Polo. Campo San Polo is one of the largest squares in the city. This is the place they sometimes hold carnivals and festivals. Most of the time it is relatively uncrowded and quiet with a handful of cafés dotted around the perimeter. A good place to have a break from the crowds in high season. The church of San Polo sits in the centre, as does the well. On the eastern side is the beautiful Gothic Palazzo Soranzo.

Campo San Polo

To exit the square, continue past the church from where you came in, keeping the church on your right, past the church tower and over a bridge into Calle dei Saoneri. Take the second right into Calle Seconda dei Saoneri following signs for Piazzale Roma. As it widens out at the end, take a left into Rio Tera Cazza and follow to a bridge. Turn right just before the bridge and go over the next bridge to the Frari on the opposite side.

11 Frari. What a spectacular church and square it is from this angle, see small picture above. I love this little piazza with a canal and the shops running along the opposite side. One of the nicest in Venice I think. It can be a good place to sit and ponder, watch gondolas go by, and maybe have a bite of alfresco lunch.

The Frari church – massive inside

The church is the largest and one of the three most important churches in Venice. The imposing edifice built of brick in the Italian Gothic style, was completed in 1338. Plain on the outside, but it houses many works of art on the inside, including some major works by Titian. The building next door is a former monastery. Opening times. The church is open from 9am-6pm Mon-Sat, and 1pm-6pm Sun. Entrance fee, €3 for adults.

To get to the Scuola Grande di San Rocco, go around to the other side of the church, past the tower, then turn right where you will find the Scuola on the left at the end of a small square.

12   Scuola Grande di San Rocco. The Scuola Grande di San Rocco is a lay confraternity founded in 1478. It is a unique site, where more than sixty paintings are preserved in their original setting in a building that has hardly undergone any alteration since its construction. Don't forget to use the mirrors to see the paintings on the ceiling. See more in Chapter 2.

There is a little diversion here to Campo San Pantalon. If you have not been here on one of the other walks, it is very worthwhile. To get there, in the square outside, you will see a small entrance on the right among the shops with a sign to

Scuola Grande di San Rocco

Accademia and San Marco. Follow it, going over a bridge, taking a right at the end then an immediate left, arriving at Campo San Pantalon at the end.

13   Campo and church of San Pantalon This is a lovely little square, like a patio surrounded by the canal with old buildings, some in a better shape than others; but it is part of the character. The church does not look like much from the outside, but the star of the show is the awe-

Campo San Pantalon

inspiring dark painted ceiling with its illusionistic effects. It is one of the largest paintings ever created. This is a hidden gem. Opening times. The church is open from 10am-noon and 3.30pm-6pm Mon-Sat, entrance is free.

Follow your steps back to the San Rocco, turning left past the gallery, taking the alley on the left at the end of the square to the end of the next little square. Take a right and an immediate left round the shop ahead into Calle Chiovere and over a bridge into Calle dei Amai, which is even narrower. At the end is a small square; turn left along the canal where you will find the Tolentini just around the corner.

86

14   Tolentini. (Full name: Chiesa di San Nicola da Tolentino). A small church built between 1591 and 1602, overlooking a plain piazza with an attractive canal and streets of cafés and restaurants in the immediate vicinity. Opening times. 8.30-noon and 4.30pm-6.30pm Mon-Sat, and 4.30pm-6.30pm Sun.

15   Back to Piazzale Roma. From the Tolentini, turn right and follow this attractive canal with its restaurants and cafés until you reach the Grand Canal. Find one of the bars for a beer on the way back. At the Grand Canal, turn left over the bridge and follow it to Piazzale Roma where you started. Another trip round one of the most interesting neighbourhoods of Venice completed.

The Tolentini church

Busy morning on the Cannaregio Canal

The Casino lit up at night next to the Grand Canal

Early morning – locals at the Rialto Markets

Chapter 8 - Getting Out and About - Cannaregio & Murano

Cannaregio & Murano - the area

Cannaregio and Murano are two areas situated to the north side the Grand Canal. Murano is a separate island about a couple of kilometres away from the main city, but it makes a nice boat trip. Other than the main drag to St Mark's and the same in Murano, both areas are much quieter residential neighbourhoods and more relaxing to explore, especially in the evening. Most of the crowds in Murano are around the boat stations to Burano and people going to view the glass works.

Tranquil Cannaregio

The first communities became established in Cannaregio in the 15th century, and were more planned than the medieval areas of San Marco and San Polo, with long straight canals giving easier access. The long canals are some of the prettiest in Venice. Strada Nova, the main route from the station to the Rialto and St Mark's, was created in 1871 by filling in canals and gaps right through the neighbourhood. Over a third of the local population of Venice lives in Cannaregio.

Long picturesque canals

The main sights are the churches of Madonna dell'Orto, Miracoli and Gesuiti, then the Jewish Ghetto (Ghetto Nuovo), and finally the gallery and palazzo at Ca' d'Oro. This is a good place to get a gondola ride so you can experience both the backwaters and the Grand Canal, including going under the Rialto Bridge.

There are a number of interesting restaurants with canal side dinning, which can make for a romantic summer evening. The area also comes alive at night with live music and happy hours in some of the bars, including Timon, Al Parlamento and Paradiso Perduto.

Murano, a group of small islands focused on glass making with a number of active workshops, is much lower key than the main city of Venice. The Rio dei Vetrai has many glass shops on both sides of the canal, selling amazing pieces that may be a bit cheaper than around St Mark's; but there is also a lot of foreign stuff, so be aware.

Hot work in the glassworks

The walk

This walk will take you on a trip showing you the best of the neighbourhood, including the Campo Ghetto Nuovo and zigzagging along the three main canals. Starting at Piazzale Roma, we follow the Grand Canal along the station side where there are wonderful views of the architecture on the opposite side on the way to the Scalzi Bridge. Head left along the Canale di Cannaregio, away from the main drag and hordes of grockles, and in 5 minutes, through a couple of back streets, you'll reach the Campo Ghetto Nuovo, the centre of the Jewish community. Early morning is a good time as many of the delivery boats are in action with plenty of activity along this canal.

Quiet back streets of Murano

Early morning shopping

From the Campo Ghetto, we zigzag along all three main canals, which can be confusing as they all look amazing and exactly the same. It's a good place to stop off for a coffee and take in some canal side ambiance. Well recommended. The route along the canals takes in the church of Madonna dell'Orto and then Fondamenta Misericordia before arriving at the church of Gesuiti.

The scene then opens out as we head onto the promenade of the Fondamente Nove, with fantastic views of the northern Lagoon. Here we pick up the boat to Murano, passing the cemetery island of San Michele. On reaching Murano, head for a glass works and experience the art of glass blowing before wandering along the Fondamenta dei Vetrai to see some of the amazing glass ornaments which have been made. There are also many shops selling traditional lace.

Taking the boat back to the city, we then visit one of the most important churches in Venice, the Santi Giovanni e Paolo. From here we head off to see a couple more churches and campos at Santa Maria del Miracoli and Santi Apostoli before arriving at palazzo Ca' d'Oro which is a traditional Venetian palace. From here you can either head off in the southerly direction to the Rialto Bridge or take the No.1 vaporetto back to Piazzale Roma. Ca' d'Oro is also a good place for a gondola ride.

Quiet backwaters – Cannaregio

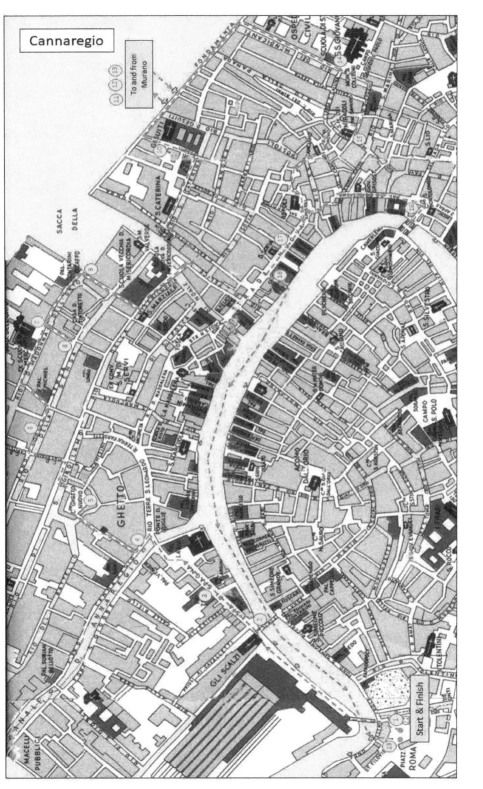

What's en route?

To start the walk, head for Piazzale Roma. The best way to get around is to follow the map carefully. If you get lost, don't despair, go back to the last place and try again. Wherever you are, if you have time, just have a wander around the immediate area you are in. To help you visualise and navigate, the small pictures below are the views you will see on the walk.

1 Piazzale Roma. This is the starting and finishing point. Not the best place to be initiated in the glories of Venice, as it doesn't feel like you are there quite yet. But I can assure you, it will only get better from here. If you don't have these already, best to stop at the Tourist Information to get yourself a map and a boat ticket for the vaporetto, and buy supplies from the supermarket by the Grand Canal before you set off.

Scalzi Bridge from Piazzale Roma

When you are ready, head off over the new bridge, Ponte della Costituzione, and along the Grand Canal past the station. This side of the canal starts to give you a perspective of old Venice along the opposite bank of the Grand Canal, a good place to take a few photographs. You may be lucky and see the Orient Express in the station. But certainly, you will also be joined by the hordes of day trippers from the station heading for St Mark's Square, though that won't last long. As you walk along the promenade, you will see the Scalzi Bridge ahead.

2 Scalzi Bridge. The Scalzi Bridge is one of four major crossing points along the Grand Canal. Just next to the bridge is the Chiesa di Santa Maria di Nazareth (known as the Scalzi), worth having a look if it is open, as most people miss it. The top of the bridge is a good place to take a photograph or the first 'selfie', giving the long perspective of the Grand Canal and the amazing architecture on both sides. It is worth spending a few moments here taking it all in.

From the bottom of the bridge, follow the hordes of ants continuing on the same side of the canal. This will take you into Lista di Spagna.

Scalzi Bridge

3   Lista di Spagna. Lista di Spagna is a main tourist street full of cheap souvenir shops, budget hotels and grotty bars - not the best of Venice. Wander along to the far end into Campo San Geremia, which is an attractive square with the Palazzo Labia. You can go in here to look at the frescos but will need to phone in advance for an appointment. It used to be a prestigious palace built by the Labia family, who were merchants, but it has been passed from owner to owner over the years and much of the original glitz has now gone.

Lista di Spagna

Continue to the far corner of the square, then along the street of more tourist shops with cheap tack and three-day old pizzas for sale, to the bridge. Go over the bridge and turn left along Fondamenta Cannaregio.

4   Fondamenta Cannaregio. The bridge is a good place to take a photograph of this picturesque canal and busy work boats early in the morning. The other good way to get an interesting photograph is to take one from the vaporettos which come this way (No.4 or 5 from Piazzale Roma to Fondamenta Nuove and Murano). Sadly, it is here we have to leave the crowds to find their own way to St Mark's. This is an interesting street of local shops, restaurants and cafés with a lot going on. More so first thing in the morning, where the whole place is really busy when all the boats come in to unload. This is where we enter the real Cannaregio, which has much more of a local feel. It's worth wandering along here if you have time, as we will be turning off soon.

About 100 metres from the bridge, just before house 1122, there is an entrance like a doorway leading into Calle Ghetto Vecchio, which will take you into another world, like Alice when she goes through

View of the Cannaregio Canal

93

the looking glass. You are now in the Jewish quarter. Follow it straight through a couple of small squares over a canal, where you may see the washing hanging out. You have now arrived at Campo Ghetto Nuovo.

5   Ghetto Nuovo. Life stills goes on in this amazing square, though not so many people live here now. This square is the hub of the Jewish community, where they have been living since the 12th century. The Jews were segregated in 1516, a curfew was imposed and they were gated in at night; see Chapter 2. This place used to be a hive of industry and workshops, as well as a number of synagogues, so was very overcrowded - hence the high-rise living. If you look at the square from

Local life in the Ghetto

the north, you can see the Scuola Italiana synagogue and its wooden cupola of 1575 on top of the private apartments. Very often you can still see the locals playing football in the square, even though it is banned by the laws of Venice. There is a museum, Museo Ebraico, and a synagogue tour. Opening times. 10am-7pm (5.30pm Oct to May) Sun-Fri, entrance fee, €8 for adults or €12 with tour.

The Ghetto – Early morning light

From here, we are now going to see all three long canals on the way to the Madonna dell'Orto. From the campo, head across to the far corner, going over the canal bridge, then right. This is the first of the three long canals, the Fondamenta dei Ormesini. There are lovely little cafés along all these canals. Pass a café, then take the left at the next bridge going down a narrow alley, Calle de la Malvasia, and over the bridge to the next canal at the end, which will give you a stunning view. Here you may find the best Venice washing strung across the alleyways. You are now on the second of the three canals, the Fondamenta della Sensa.

6   Fondamenta della Sensa. When the marsh lands of the Cannaregio were drained, these three long straight canals were created. Fondamenta della Sensa is the central one of the three. It can be confusing as they all look the same. They are all as picturesque as each other. This is a quieter quarter where daily life timelessly goes on, not disturbed by tourism as you can see by the locals going about their business. Here you will find small grocery shops and

simple local bars. A good place to stop for a coffee and watch the world go by, or experience the romance of canal side dining in the evening with candle-lit tables or the local snacks in the cicheti bars, such as Vino Vero.

From the bridge, head along the canal to the right, going over a bridge. Just past the bridge, turn left into a very narrow alley, Calle Loredan, and follow over the wooden bridge at the end. You have now reached the third canal. Turn right and follow down to the square and church of Madonna dell'Orto.

Fondamenta della Sensa

7   Madonna dell'Orto. This is a richly decorated Gothic church containing works by Tintoretto; he was buried here, one of Venice's best kept secrets. Opening times. 10am-5pm Mon-Sat, entrance fee, €3 for adults.

To find Campo Mori, take the bridge over the canal opposite the Madonna dell'Orto and it is about a minute down the alley.

Madonna dell'Orto

8   Campo dei Mori. This little square has a couple of canal side cafés and restaurants which give you another view of the Fondamenta della Sensa. From here retrace your steps back to the Madonna dell'Orto, and turn right along the main canal Fondamenta Madonna dell'Orto. Continue to where it ends at the harbour, Sacca della Misericordia.

Campo dei Mori

9 Sacca della Misericordia. This is a large man-made basin which overlooks the northern Lagoon giving you a bit of space and air from the cramped alleyways. Looking across the Lagoon there are views of Murano and the cemetery on San Michele.

Cross the bridge and continue down Corte Vecchia, over the bridge opposite into Calle Trevisan. Go to the end, then turn left. We are now back on the first canal, Fondamenta della Misericordia. Continue along the canal, over a bridge, where next you will find a little bridge without a parapet. This is one of only two in Venice. Get someone to take your photo standing on this bridge from the one next door. Don't fall off. Continue over the bridge through the doorway opposite. It's very dark in here. When you come out into the

Sacca della Misericordia

daylight, turn left along Calle Racheta, then take a right after the next bridge alongside the canal. Go to the end and turn left through a small square. You will then see the impressive white stone pillars of the Gesuiti on your right.

10 Gesuiti. This church is different from some of the others. It has a stunning interior of inlaid white and green marble which looks like wallpaper. The ceiling is made of gold and white stuccowork, all of which makes an amazing impact, completely different from what you would expect from the outside. You will also find Titian's Martyrdom of St Lawrence on the left as you enter the church. Opening times. 10am-noon and 3.30pm-5pm Mon-Sat, entrance fee, €1 for adults.

To get to Murano, turn right out of the church to the vaporetto jetties on the Fondamenta Nuove. Take the No.4.1 or 4.2 to the Colonna waterbus stop, which will take about 10-15 minutes.

Gesuiti

11 Vaporetto to Murano. The trip will take you out into the Lagoon. On the way you will get a close-up view of the cemetery island of San Michele. It's a good time to either rest your feet or take some interesting photos of the Venice skyline from the back of the boat.

12 Murano glass factories. Murano is famous for making glass, but the most interesting glass factories on Murano are not open to visitors as they are in the business of making glass, not entertaining tourists, and the real art is also secret squirrel. Master glass artisans have spent years refining their proprietary techniques and operate in secrecy to protect the brand. Glass making was moved to Murano after a decree in 1291 stating that glass making was hazardous and that there was a high risk of setting people's houses on fire, so it was

Master at work

Entrance to the Fornace

isolated. But still, as you walk around Murano, you're likely to find mass-market fornaci or furnaces that welcome tourists, such as the V.I.A factory near the Colonna stop or the Glass Factory Colleoni at the other end of the main canal.

To find the V.I.A factory, turn left as you exit the Colonna boat platform at the waterbus stop and walk alongside the water until you reach a 'Fornace Glass' sign on a door below the Calle S. Cipriano street sign, about 5-10 minutes away. Pass beneath the Fornace - Entrata Libera' entrance sign, follow the pavement, and enter the factory to view a free glass making demonstration (afterwards, you'll exit through the showroom). The demonstration takes less than 10 minutes, but it's interesting if you haven't seen a glass furnace.

A couple of tips for visiting the glass factories:
- Look for open factories on weekday mornings. Don't count on much action during the lunch hour (which can run from noon until mid-afternoon).
- Glass factories are not normally open during August.
- Real Murano glass is expensive. Many of the stores and warehouses are packed with imitations made in the Far East.

Murano glass – Wonderful creations

97

- As you come off the boat, you may get approached by representatives of various glass shops trying to get you into their stores; ignore them.
- Finally, at your hotel, you're likely to be approached by representatives of touristy factory showrooms that offer free boat trips to Murano. If you accept, be prepared for a high-pressure sales pitch. It is much better to go by public transport and be under your own control, which is easy and pressure free.

13   Murano. From the Colonna waterbus stop, take a right and follow round to the main street Fondamenta dei Vetrai. Here is where you will find many glass and lace shops, many selling imported goods. Fornace Gino Mazzuccato has an amazing showroom upstairs if you can get in. To do this, go over the little bridge and find a small alleyway with a door at end - if they let you in, they do a demo for a tip of around €10. This is where they normally bring top-end tours which come in by water taxi.

Fondamenta dei Vetrai

A slow wander along the street will give you a different perspective of this island compared with the main city of Venice. Much lower key, but full of interesting shops and cafés. Sometimes there are also some glass sculptures by the clock tower at the end. If you wish to go to the Glass Factory Colleoni, cross over the bridge by the clock tower and Calle Santo Stefano, then follow the water round for 5 to 10 minutes.

Otherwise follow round to the left to the Murano Da Mula waterbus stop for either a No.4.1 or 4.2 vaporetto. Or, if you want to explore the far side, go over the bridge and take the same vaporetto from the Ferry Terminal Museo stop.

Murano – from Riva Longa

The vaporetto will take you back to Fondamenta Nuova, offering another chance to take photographs of the Venice skyline on the way. Front entrance of the boat is best this time. On getting there, continue along the promenade over a couple of bridges and turn right into Fondamenta Mendicanti. Follow to the end past the Ospeddale Civile, which was one of Venice's original confraternities, to arrive at Campo Giovanni e Paolo.

14   Santi Giovanni e Paolo (San Zanipolo). This church is situated in a wonderful square; it's well worth having a break here sitting in the sunshine to take it all in. Next door to the church is the Scuola Grande di San Marco where the library is worth a visit if you have time. In the centre is the bronze statue of a horse, the Statue of Bartolomeo Colleoni. Church opening times. 9am-6pm Mon-Sat and noon-6pm Sun, entrance fee, €2.50 for adults.

Giovanni e Paolo

Leave the square down the side of canal, taking a right over the bridge into Calle de le Erbe. Here we enter the narrow alleys of old Venice. Go over the next bridge, taking a right followed by an immediate left down Calle Castelli where the church of Santa Maria dei Miracoli can be found at the end on the right, a beautiful sight.

15   Santa Maria dei Miracoli. This marble-clad church is an amazing piece of architecture, built from marble scavenged from the San Marco slag heaps. It is a masterpiece of Renaissance engineering. The inside is as stunning as the outside. This is one of the jewels in Venice's crown, squirrelled away and hard to find. The canal scenes are also very pretty round here and it is worth walking round the outside of the church and having a drink in the café in the square opposite. Opening times. 10.30am-4.30pm Mon-Sat, entrance fee, €3 for adults.

Church of Miracoli from the square

Church of Miracoli – the entrance

Turn left out of the church, then down the side of the church and left over the bridge at the end into Campo Santa Maria Nova, a delightful little square overlooking the church. A good place for some photographs. Exit the square at the far end to the left into Calle dei Spezier and take an immediate right into Campiello S. Canciano. Follow Campiello S. Canciano over the bridge and through the next campo into another narrow alley. At the next campo, bear left and go out through the opposite corner down the alley; you will suddenly exit through a gap in the walls into free space. You have now arrived in Campo Apostoli and the hordes of tourists again. Two different worlds just meters apart.

If you wish to go to the shops at Campo San Bartolomeo and the Rialto Bridge, follow the Rialto signs and then return here. Otherwise continue across the square into Strada Nova.

Miracoli to Campo Apostoli

Campo Apostoli to San Bartolomeo and Rialto Bridge.

16 San Bartolomeo and Rialto Bridge. A lively place with lots of shops here as the alleys open out into the Campo. This square is hidden away, but it is just next door to the Rialto Bridge. If you want to browse in even more shops, continue to the opposite end of the square into Merceria, one of the premium shopping streets on the main drag up from St Mark's Square.

Sunset behind the Rialto Bridge

To find the Rialto Bridge, take an exit on the right along Salizzada Pio X and you will reach the bridge in one minute. Before you go up over the bridge, it is worth taking a left along Riva Ferro along the bank of the Grand Canal and taking in some of the views along there. There are also a few restaurants if you want to choose one with a view right on the Grand Canal.

17 Strada Nova. Back at Campo Apostoli, you are now on the main tourist drag up from the station to Piazza San Marco. This is part of one of the longest tourist streets in Venice, another opportunity to buy imported cheap stuff. Possibly a plastic gold plated Rialto Bridge or a hat. Maybe time to have a dodgy burger. Follow this

Strada Nova and all its crowds

street for about 200 metres until you find the narrow alley, Calle Ca' d'Oro, on the left. It is hard to find, but there is a yellow sign directing you there. You will find the gallery on the right and the vaporetto stop for the way back at the far end at the Grand Canal.

18   Ca' d'Oro. The Galleria Giorgio Franchetti alla Ca' d'Oro is one of the showcases on the Grand Canal. It is one of the most beautiful buildings, built in the 15th century, and one of Venice's most splendid Gothic palazzos. It is full of masterpieces, many of which Napoleon plundered from Venice's churches. Opening times. 8.15am-2pm Mon and 8.15am-7.15pm Tue-Sun, entrance fee, €8.50 for adults.

Ca' d'Oro

19   Back to Piazzale Roma. Ca' d'Oro is a good place to take a gondola ride. Here they tend to do a loop which is partly in the back-alley network of canals and then up the Grand Canal under the Rialto Bridge, which makes it even more exciting. Tell them where you want to go.

Sunset over the Grand Canal

From the Ca' d'Oro waterbus stop, take the No.1 vaporetto up the Grand Canal towards the station and Piazzale Roma. You are back where you started, a day well spent with no annoying red flags or hopefully umbrellas to follow, and you'll have seen something of Venice most tourists miss out on or never see.

Downtown Murano

Chapter 9 - Getting Out and About - Dorsoduro & Giudecca

Dorsoduro and Giudecca - the area

Dorsoduro and Giudecca are the two areas situated to the south side of the city, the Dorsoduro on the edge of the Grand Canal opposite St Mark's, and Giudecca, a separate island south of the Dorsoduro across the water from the main city, which provides spectacular views across the Giudecca Canal. They are much quieter than San Marco and more pleasant to wander around. Dorsoduro, with its bars and its beautiful views of the Lagoon from the Zattere, makes for a good evening stroll. You will find very few guided tours round here, but the architecture and the street scenes are just as beautiful as St Mark's, if not even better without the tour groups and the noise.

Pretty colours in the autumn light

It is more vibrant and busier around the Accademia Bridge and Campo Santa Margherita with the shops, cafés and restaurants and there is plenty of atmosphere. But if it is solitude you are after, the western end of the Dorsoduro is so quiet, you hardly see any tourists down there, even during the height of the season in August.

Evening fruit stalls in Dorsoduro

The Dorsoduro is named after the solid subsoil on which the area is built. The western part was colonised before the Rialto was established as a permanent seat of Venice in AD 828. East of the Accademia Bridge, the neighbourhood has quiet shaded squares and picturesque residences belonging to the wealthy Venetians.

The main sights are the Accademia and Peggy Guggenheim Galleries, the church of Santa Maria della Salute, the gondola workshop, the palace of Ca' Rezzonico, which is one of the most beautiful in Venice and only one of a handful on the Grand Canal that is open to the public, and Campo Barnaba. But my favourite is the church of San Nicolo dei Mendicoli, in a very quiet area at the very western end. From the drab unkempt appearance outside one would not guess this is one of the most amazing churches in Venice, but very few make it here. Be aware it closes at noon.

Lots of local shops – Dorsoduro

103

The walk below will take you there, where you will be rewarded.

The island of Giudecca in times gone by was an aristocratic retreat, a pleasure ground of palaces and gardens. Now it is more neglected and made up of residential apartments, slowly replacing the abandoned workshops and warehouses. The big mill warehouse, which you can see from all over Venice, has now been turned into the upmarket Hilton Molino Stucky Hotel with the popular Skyline bar which wows everyone with its panoramic views all round Venice. But the best part of the island is the promenade, which makes for an interesting walk providing stunning views of Venice, and not a bad place for a spot of lunch on a sunny day. We are going to take you there too.

Waterfront – Giudecca

The walk

This walk will take you on a trip, showing you the best of the neighbourhood, including the back streets of the Dorsoduro, with strolls along two amazing promenades, finishing at the Accademia Bridge where you can visit the Galleries or get the boat back to Piazzale Roma. Along the way you will see stunning views of the Lagoon and the Venice skyline.

Starting at Piazzale Roma, we follow a couple of canals to get to Campo Santa Margherita, which is a good place to get a cappuccino if you have not had one already. Not far is the next stop, the delightful Campo San Barnaba, hopefully with the vegetable boats and gondolas on display, before heading down a really long narrow eerie alley towards the church of San Nicolo dei

Lunch with a view – Giudecca

Mendicoli, one of the most amazing churches in Venice. Around here you are likely to have the place to yourself with very few tourists. Following the canals back to the Zattere, you can then stroll along and get the feel of this beautiful promenade, have a beer at one of the bars, then look at the gondola workshop before taking the boat to Giudecca.

Once on Giudecca you can get the full perspective of the Venice skyline,

Nicked! – at the Salute

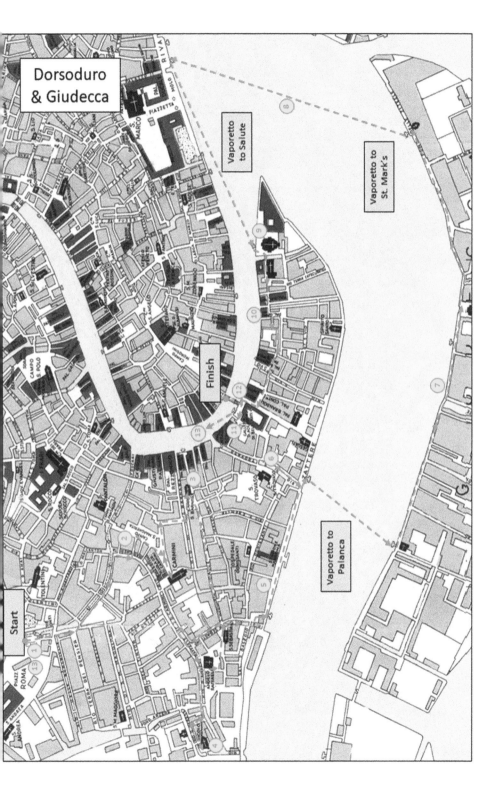

Dorsoduro & Giudecca

including the Salute and the grand Campanile at St Mark's all in one view. We walk the whole length of this enchanting promenade. From Giudecca, it is a short boat ride to St Mark's and a hop back to the Salute, stopping off at St Mark's if you so wish.

After visiting this wonderful church, we then follow the back alleys and squares past the Peggy Guggenheim Collection to the Accademia Bridge and Galleries. You can either go on from here or take the No.1 vaporetto back to Piazzale Roma.

Where there's a will, there's a way

What's en route?

To start the walk, head for Piazzale Roma. The best way to get around is to follow the map carefully. If you get lost, go back to the last place and try again. Wherever you are, if you have time, just have a wander around the immediate area you are in. To help you visualise and navigate, the small pictures below are the views you will see on the walk.

1   Piazzale Roma. This is the starting and finishing point. Not a good place, but you are not in real Venice yet, it will only get better from here. But best to stop at the Tourist Information, get yourself a map, a boat ticket for the vaporetto and supplies from the supermarket by the Grand Canal before you set off. For this walk we are going to head out of Piazzale Roma a different way.

Rio Nuovo towards Piazzale Roma

From the new Constitution Bridge, face up the Grand Canal, and in about 20 metres, take the first right around the Hotel, along the first large canal. You follow a narrow park separating the canal from the bus station to the red brick bridge (third bridge) where the canal splits, passing a stone bridge and a wooden bridge on the way. The street scene gets a lot better with some little restaurants on the canal side. Cross the red brick bridge and turn right along Fondamenta Rio Nuovo, keeping the second canal on your left, passing some unfortunate new buildings on the way, until the corner at the end. Follow round to the right and turn left over the second (red brick) bridge, going straight through the narrow alley, Calle del Forno, which will take you neatly into Campo Santa Margherita.

Typical restaurant – Campo Margherita

2   Campo Santa Margherita. This is one of the most notable and largest campos in Venice; see 'Piazzas and campos' in Chapter 2. It is a hive of activity, both day and night. A good place to enjoy a coffee in the sunshine or dinner later in the evening. The Scuola Grande dei Carmini is worth a visit and can be found down the far end of the campo on the right, along with the church of Santa Maria dei Carmini next door, which is a hidden gem. Opening times. Scuola Grande dei Carmini 11am-5pm, entrance fee €5, and church of Santa Maria dei Carmini 8am-noon, 2.30pm-5.30pm Mon-Sat; 4pm-6.30pm Sun, entrance fee, free.

From where you entered, head down the campo following the fork to the left into a narrow street then turn right into a wide street with interesting shops and cafés. Go over the bridge at the end and follow the canal left and you will arrive in Campo San Barnaba. Look at the amazing view from the bridge on the way.

Lively stalls – Campo Margherita

3   Campo San Barnaba. See Chapter 2, 'Piazzas and campos'. This campo has one of the loveliest natural views in Venice. Amazing photos of the church with the campanile behind can be taken from many vantage points. Hopefully, there'll be some gondolas too and the vegetable boat added to the mix. The square also has a couple of nice cafés. Opening times. The church is open from 9.30am to 7.30pm daily, entrance fee, free.

Campo San Barnaba

Head west out of the back of the square into Calle Lunga San Barnaba, going over the bridge at the end straight on into Calle Avogaria. Calle Lunga San Barnaba is an amazing long narrow alley which can make you feel claustrophobic but also offers some good photographic opportunities. Just before the church at the end, turn right before the bridge along the canal to the next bridge at the end into Fondamenta San Sebastiano. Follow round to the right in a 'U' over the bridge to the canal on the opposite side, into Fondamenta Briati, coming back on yourself. Pass two bridges and take the next right into Calle Rielo. Go to the end and follow along the canal to the left, Calle San Nicolo, and you will arrive at an interesting little square and the church at the end on your left. A little unkempt and a bit of weeding needed, but it's very quiet and peaceful down here.

4   San Nicolo dei Mendicoli. I think this is one of the most beautiful churches in Venice, but you may not think so from the outside. Go inside, it's very old and it's wonderful, and you are likely to be the only people there. It has appeared in a couple of films and is the second oldest church in Venice. Opening times. The church is open from 10am-noon and 3pm-5.30pm Mon-Sat and 9am-noon Sun.

From the church, retrace your route back to Fondamenta Briati, taking the second of the two bridges to the right which you passed on the way down. Go past the large white church on your left. If you fancy a bit of solitude from the hectic life elsewhere, there are a couple of bars along Fondamenta Briati, where you sit outside and lose yourself in your thoughts over a couple of beers. Turn left into Campo de l'Anzolo Rafael, where

San Nicolo dei Mendicoli

there is a lone restaurant which is supposed to be very good. See more in Chapter 2, 'Piazzas and campos'. Bearing towards the right, follow through the next couple of squares going over the bridge by the church opposite. After the bridge turn right, continuing down to the Lagoon, where via another attractive square, you are at the start of the Zattere.

5   Zattere. A lovely place to take in the fresh air on the water front. Here we meander down most of the promenade, stopping at as many of the hostelries as you like. Normally one can spend a couple of hours here on a good day. On the opposite side you can see Giudecca, where we will be going soon.

Promenade – Zattere

Dorsoduro backwaters

Continue down the Zattere to the next bridge that goes over a canal (a little way down). Turn immediately left along the canal and you will be at San Trovaso and the gondola workshops.

6   San Trovaso and gondola workshop. The Squero (boatyard) di San Trovaso is a small gondola boatyard that first opened in the 17th century. Back in the 16th century, heyday of the gondola, there were upwards of 10,000 of these elegant boats plying the waters of Venice's canals. Today there are but 350.

Gondola workshops – San Trovaso

Go back to the Zattere where you will get a fantastic view of the Lagoon again, turning left to find the Zattere vaporetto station a few metres down. Take a No.2, 4.1 or 4.2 vaporetto scheduled to San Marco in an easterly direction to cross the water, one stop to Palanca boat station. You are now on the island of Giudecca.

7   Giudecca. This is a lovely quiet island, the best part being the promenade, which we are going to walk most of, heading east from the vaporetto station. The main attraction is the wonderful views of Venice, including the Campanile at St Mark's Square with the dome of the Salute in the foreground. Giudecca is a good place to find a waterside restaurant for lunch about halfway along. Also look at the church of Santissimo Redenlore.

Promenade – Giudecca

Continue along the promenade to the second vaporetto station, Zielle, where we take a No.2, 4.1 or 4.2 scheduled to San Marco in an easterly direction.

8   Vaporetto to San Marco. The boat trip to San Marco will be a real experience. You will get grandstand views of the island and church tower of San Giorgio Maggiore, then a waterside view of the Doge's Palace, the Campanile and the Riva degli Schiavoni at St Mark's. Be sure to take plenty of pictures as the journey is relatively quick and there will be plenty of action in the Lagoon.

From St Mark's, take the No.1 vaporetto in the direction of Piazzale Roma a couple of stops to the Salute.

Busy waters – beware of other ferries!

9   Santa Maria Salute. The third of the three most important churches in Venice along with the Basilica and the Frari. But this great Baroque church is the one most represented in paintings and photographs, standing at the entrance to the Grand Canal. It was built in thanks to the deliverance of the city from the plague and was completed in 1687. Inside it is quite sober, but has

The Salute from the Accademia Bridge

some works of art near the altar and on the ceiling. Opening times. From 9am to noon and 3pm to 5.30pm, entrance fee €3 for adults.

From the Salute, take the first bridge over the canal into Calle dei Bastion. Follow through a couple of squares and over a bridge, where you bear round to the left and then right into Campiello Barbaro. The entrance to the Peggy Guggenheim Collection will be found through a little gateway on the corner.

10   Peggy Guggenheim Collection.
Heiress Peggy Guggenheim made
art history by changing her palatial
home, Palazzo Venier dei Leoni,
into a place for modern art. She
collected   works   covering
surrealism, futurism and abstract
art from nearly 200 breakthrough
modern artists, some who were
rumoured to be her lovers. The
works include *The Poet* by Pablo
Picasso. Never afraid to be
controversial, Peggy placed a
bronze male nude on horseback
outside on her Grand Canal quay,
which gave the passing gondoliers
an eyeful and excitement for their
passengers.

Peggy Guggenheim – on the banks of the Grand
Canal

To get to the Accademia, turn right
out of the gate, and follow right along the bank of the canal at the end, a pretty
little stretch. Continue straight on down a narrow alley, over a bridge, into
Campo San Vio. There are very often sculptures here, and certainly good views
of the Grand Canal. Go over the bridge and continue straight on and you will
soon reach the Accademia. The entrance is round on the opposite side.

11   Gallery Accademia. If you are
into art, or not into art but have
time, this is one of the must do's,
even if you visit no other gallery,
and if only because of its
surroundings. It is one of the top
art galleries in Venice, which
traces the development of
Venetian art from the 14th to the
18th centuries, with works by
Bellini,   Titian,   Tintoretto,
Veronese and Canaletto among
others.   It   includes   Paolo
Veronese's *Feast in the House
of Levi*. It is open from 8.15am
to 2pm on Mondays and from

Gallery Accademia – One of the best

8.15am to 7.15pm the rest of the week. There can be a long queue in the
summer and busy periods, so it is advisable to get an advanced booking to
reserve your time by either calling the main number +39 041 520 0345 or via
www.gallerieaccademia.org. Entry costs are €12 plus a €1.50 advanced
reservation fee.

The Accademia Bridge is just next door.

12 Accademia Bridge. This bridge is one of the four main bridges over the Grand Canal; see Chapter 2. A good place to take photographs of classic views as the old masters saw them. Also a place to watch the activity on the Grand Canal passing underneath.

13 Back to Piazzale Roma finishing with a ride up the Grand Canal. From the vaporetto station at the bridge, take the No.1 vaporetto up the Grand Canal towards the station and Piazzale Roma. At night, it is a magical experience not to be missed. The back of the boat is the best view. At the end, you are back where you started, a day well spent seeing some of the more remote and interesting sights of Venice without so many crowds. If you liked Campo Margherita, find a nice restaurant there for dinner.

Grand Canal – boat side view

Castello and the Lagoon in the evening light from the Campanile

The Basilica at night

St Mark's on a warm spring evening

Chapter 10 – Where to Stay, Eat, Drink, Spend Your Money and Have Fun

Deciding where to stay, what to do and where to eat in Venice is a minefield because there is so much choice, and most of it is not bad. For those of us who are indecisive, it can send our minds into a tizzy. Much of it is down to your taste and what you enjoy. It's all about having fun, and not just to be seen on Facebook having a €500 meal, which is quite easily done round here. An expensive picture I would say! It all makes making a decision that much more difficult. Hopefully the views and considerations from experience in this chapter will make it easier for you.

There are many recommendations around; the latest online reviews tend to be best as they are more up to date (check the date). Papers and magazines also do periodic reviews on Venice; check the web. But in a book, they go out of date with time, so I am not going to make any

Explore the back alleys

On the move

recommendations here, but just show you what Venice has to offer, and how to go about finding what you want. Sometimes, it is best to just wander down the street with an open mind and find somewhere you like when you get there, particularly for restaurants - it is much more interesting and satisfying. And from my experience, many of the lower ranked ones are just as good as those at the top of the list; they can have a better

ambiance and provide a more authentic experience of real Venice. Just compare difference in recommendations on TripAdvisor with leading guide books and you will see what I mean. Who is right? Even more confused now?

To start, there are many review websites to choose from, not just TripAdvisor. UK national papers, such as the *Telegraph*, *Independent* and *Guardian*, regularly make recommendations. Then there are a host of travel websites, and local Venice sites.

Cases on the move, hopefully not falling in

Venice – Eating, Bars & Shopping

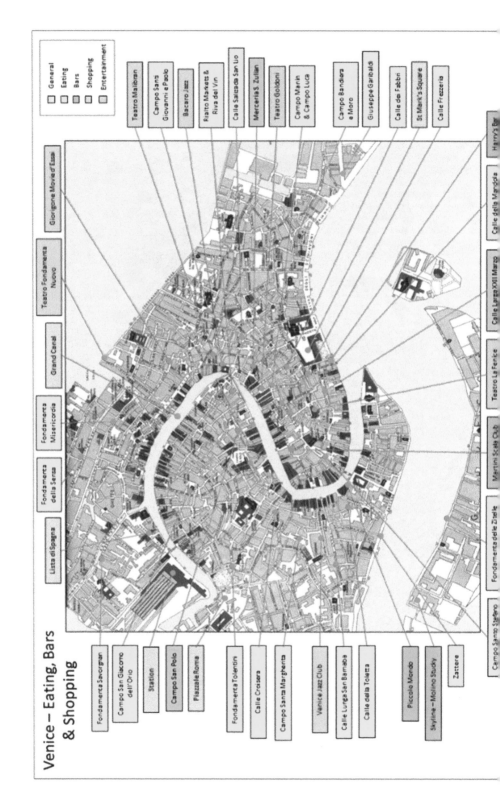

Legend:
- General
- Eating
- Bars
- Shopping
- Entertainment

Labels: Teatro Malibran, Campo Santi Giovanni e Paolo, Bacaro Jazz, Rialto Markets & Riva del Vin, Calle Salizada San Lio, Mercerias S. Zulian, Teatro Goldoni, Campo Manin & Campo Luca, Campo Bandiera e Moro, Giuseppe Garibaldi, Calle dei Fabbri, St Mark's Square, Calle Frezzeria

Giorgione Movie d'Essai, Teatro Fondamenta Nuovo, Grand Canal, Fondamenta Misericordia, Fondamenta della Sensa, Lista di Spagna

Harry's Bar, Calle delle Mandola, Calle Larga XXII Marzo, Teatro La Fenice, Martini Scala Club, Fondamenta delle Zitelle, Campo Santo Stefano

Fondamenta Savorgnan, Campo San Giacomo dell'Orio, Station, Campo San Polo, Piazzale Roma, Fondamenta Tolentini, Calle Crosera, Campo Santa Margherita, Venice Jazz Club, Calle Lunga San Barnaba, Calle della Toletta, Piccolo Mondo, Skyline – Molino Stucky, Zattere

There are specialist sites for food and others for accommodation with various biases. You also have to be careful as some are sponsored entries and others are the opinion of the author to support the picture of Venice they are trying to portray. Your best bet is to go onto Google and see what comes out - far more interesting.

Bridge of Sighs

So, this chapter concentrates on what Venice has to offer and, to save you time, provides some suggestions on how to find a place that suits you, and where they are generally located in the city. For some, cheap and rustic is good, while others want the glitz of the poo-pah expensive Hotel Danieli or the Gritti Palace. Everyone's needs, budget and perspective are different.

Where to Stay

Venice has everything from top-end luxury grandiose establishments at over €1000 a night to soulless, cheap motorway boxes with very basic facilities on the Mestre. So, what is best? Here are a few things to think about.

Some hotels have an extraordinary view

On or off the island. Staying off the island may be cheaper, but you will have to travel further and join the hordes of day trippers each day to see the city, rather than just walk out of the front door. By staying on the island, you can experience the feeling and the architecture of the past by staying in an old building. But accommodation on the island for the same price as further afield tends to be more rustic, with smaller rooms and more basic facilities (lack of space means you'll have a shower but no bath tub). By not staying on the island, you will miss out on the ambiance and the atmosphere of the city in the evening, a gentle wander along the promenade, a few bars, or trip up the Grand Canal at night. It's about the whole experience and in my view for a few extra euros, it's worth it.

Londra Palace – Expensive too!

Accommodation and prices. Venice has a lot to offer from the high-end grand palaces down to budget hotels and hostels, Airbnb or rooms people let. A number have private gardens and canal views. But many lower-end and mid-range places

117

Rialto Markets next to the Grand Canal

are not grand at all with pokey cramped rooms, dreary décor and lacklustre service, regardless of what the glowing reviews say. Choice varies enormously, from small boutique hotels with grandly furnished rooms to basic draughty hotels near the station, so beware when booking. There are plenty of B&Bs or Airbnb self-catering options. Rooms tend to range from around €100 to over €1000 a night depending on season, weekends and festival time. From early November into the spring, the prices really drop off. Wi-Fi also has difficulty penetrating the thick stone walls, so may not be available in all rooms, just the common areas - check!

Location. Location is very important for a number of reasons. If you have heavy bags, be near a vaporetto stop. Locations near the Grand Canal boat stops are best. Getting around the city, seeing the sights or popping back to your hotel can take much longer and be a pain if you have to walk far from a boat station; and it will be a lot easier to get lost at night if your accommodation is located down a dark rabbit warren of back alleys. The area around St Mark's tends to be more expensive; and anywhere with canal views will also drive up the price. Dorsoduro, Cannaregio and Castello have the best restaurants. Giudecca and the other islands are a good 30-45 minutes or more from the Rialto.

Opulence in the Danieli

Area. Each area of Venice has it pros and cons, depending on your preferences:

- San Marco. Hotels in historic buildings, optimal for sightseeing and shopping. But more expensive with smaller rooms, noisy streets and not so many good restaurants.

- Dorsoduro. Designer hotels near museums, easy access to the bars and walk along the Zattere with some good restaurants tucked away in the alleys. But further from the vaporetto stations and travel to the other sights.

- San Polo and Santa Croce. Top value boutique, mid-range hotels and B&Bs with prime location for eating and bars, shops and transport along the Grand Canal, especially near Piazzale Roma, which makes it easy to drop off your bags when you arrive. But further to walk to the main sights and beware the maze of dark back streets in trying to find your hotel at night after a few vinos.

- Cannaregio. Much quieter than the other areas, except the main drag to San Marco which has plenty of budget hotels just beyond the station in Lista di Spagna. Good for canal side happy hours and

Little boutique hotels too

restaurants with a more authentic Venetian cuisine frequented by locals. But away from the station it is a long walk and vaporetto ride to the sights around San Marco. The budget hotels can be a bit run down and noisy, and there will be the daily onslaught of people heading past for you know where.

- Castello & Giudecca. Fewer tourists and better value for money. Both have good eating with interesting restaurants on the Via Giuseppe Garibaldi in Castello and a couple on the main promenade on Giudecca. But like Cannaregio, it is a long walk and vaporetto ride to the sights around San Marco, there is little else here and you'll have a long trip back at night if eating elsewhere.

Breakfast. In many of the hotels, breakfast is extra and not good value, or not provided at all if self-catering. But do not despair, there are plenty of local cafés which are much better, especially if all you want is a coffee and a fresh croissant or two.

Little cafés for breakfast everywhere

Booking. As there are so many places to choose from, to make it easier, first decide on the area and a rough budget you want to pay. That will help narrow the choice. The internet is best both for using the review sites and for booking. It is quicker and much more reliable than printed books and articles, which tend to go out of date. In addition to review sites like TripAdvisor, local Venice review sites (use Google) and booking sites like Booking.com and Expedia, there are many others which can give you a different story and price on the same accommodation, so take a balanced view. Start with the places you like and look at the booking sites to check

Gabrielli – another posh palace hotel

and compare the cost and availability, and whether the room on offer is, first, the one you think you are getting and, second, the one you like, including amenities and canal side views. Both the review sites and the booking sites have maps where the accommodation is located and prices for given dates. Use them to narrow down your choices and to know exactly where you are staying. All this seems obvious, but so many people get disappointed when they arrive in Venice as they have not properly checked things out. Lastly, unless you don't care, to avoid

Budget hotels – Lista di Spagna

119

disappointment always book well in advance, especially at peak season or festival times. The small number of rooms in most hotels and B&Bs means the best places sell out quickly.

TOP TIP: Unless you are on a very tight budget, stay on the island. It might be more expensive, but the experience and atmosphere will more than compensate, and it is much easier to get back to your hotel and wander around after dark. From experience, it is best to prioritise spending a few more euros on better located accommodation. Just consider how much it is costing you to get to Venice and the trip overall and make savings elsewhere if budget is an issue - a much better decision you will appreciate later when you are there.

TOP TIP: Always book well in advance. The best places sell out quickly.

Discount Passes

Venice may be considered expensive, but there are a number of ways you can cut the cost and have more fun. A good place to start is Venezia Unica, the Official City of Venice Tourist and Travel Information website. www.veneziaunica.it/. It is a mine of information of what events are going on and when, and you can also create and purchase your own discount City Passes online, see below. Additionally, you can advance book tours, shows and parking, which not only guarantees you a ticket or space, but also is a saving on the turn-up-on-the-day price. The main discount options are described below. There may be further discounts if you are a student under 29 or a senior.

The back of the boat is best most of the time, maybe not when it is raining

Travelling on the vaporetto is fun and you get terrific views

Vaporetto (boat and bus tickets). A single, one-hour vaporetto trip in one direction costs €7.50 for any visitor aged 6 years and over. There are no discounts for seniors. For a person in a wheelchair, their carer can travel for €1.50 per trip. Apart from these exceptions, everyone pays full fare unless a

transport pass is used. A pass is a much better deal. Each day runs for 24 hours, and the card starts on the time and date you first use and validate the ticket. Tickets can be purchased at ACTV booths or offices, at the airport, Piazzale Roma or major stops. You can also purchase through Venezia Unica - just get a voucher and then exchange when you arrive. I tend to buy them at the airport when I arrive along with the express bus tickets to Piazzale Roma. This will

Vaporettos stop everywhere

save you time, and if you need one, you can just roll onto the boat when you arrive off the bus to go to your hotel to drop the luggage off. The cost of adult travel cards are as follows:

- €20.00 - 1 day travel card
- €30.00 - 2 days travel card
- €40.00 - 3 days travel card
- €60.00 - 7 days travel card

Grandstand views

Chorus Pass. This pass allows you entry into 16 churches within one year (except the Frari). The money goes towards the restoration of all the churches in Venice. Typically, the entry fee to a church is around €3. The cost of an adult pass is €12. Tickets can be purchased from the church ticket booths. So that's four churches to break even, but note that some are free.

The Salute

City Pass. If you are staying in Venice for any length of time, these passes cover a whole range of discounts and entry covering churches (16 Chorus churches), museums (11 civic museums, plus Querini Stampa and Jewish museum), Wi-Fi, and transport for 3 and 7 day passes. They come in Silver (churches, museums and casino only), Gold (includes 3 day transport) and Platinum (includes 7 day transport). Prices vary depending on which ticket and combinations you require. The best way to purchase is online at Venezia Unica, http://www.veneziaunica.it/, where you will get a voucher and you can pick up your tickets when you arrive. There are discounts if you are under 29.

Other passes. There are other passes and also look out for offers. It is best to look up the latest on the internet before travelling. Here are some of the other options:

- St Mark's Pass which allows entry to a number of sights and museums around St Mark's Square.

- Civic Museum Pass, allowing entry into 11 civic museums, valid for 6 months. Adult cost €24, available from civic museums.

- San Marco Pack, allowing entry into four museums around Piazza San Marco, including Palazzo Ducale. Adult cost €20, available from civic museums and the tourist office.

- St Mark's City Pass. A reduced version of the City Pass allowing entry into three civic museums on Piazza San Marco, three churches on the Chorus list and the Querini Stampa. Adult cost €20, available from civic museums and the tourist office.

View from the vaporetto

Restaurants and Cafés

Venice has everything from congealed takeaway pizza bars, to delightful cafés and Michelin-starred restaurants with expensive dining overlooking the Grand Canal. Venetians are a café culture. There is no more pleasant way to spend a day than sipping a top Italian coffee with beautiful canal and Lagoon side views. Even better if it is with breakfast. Finding a restaurant in Venice can be confusing, as during the day many restaurants or squares can look abandoned and run down, but it all comes to life at night when the shutters go up and the tables come out

Little restaurants appear everywhere at night

dressed with white tablecloths, and the place fills with people. Totally transformed. It is common for restaurant owners and waiters to stand outside and greet passers-by in the hope of drumming up trade. There's no need to worry; if you aren't interested, just say "*No, grazie*" and continue on your way. Take your time as there are so many interesting places to choose from. It is all about having a meal to remember, so here are a few ideas and things to consider.

Venetian Cuisine. Venice, like every region of Italy, is known for its traditional food specialties. Most menus are based on Italian cuisine from the region. A visit to Venice offers an opportunity to discover fascinating gastronomic delights with some of the fresh food unique to Venice, such as seafood from the Lagoon and surrounding rivers and vegetables from the Veneto, much of which can be found in the Rialto Markets. Venice does some of the best risotto made from the local salty broth of fish from the Lagoon.

Vegan & veggie menus too

Local cuisine should be your focus, which can be found in expensive restaurants with Michelin stars to the very cheapest of trattorias. Traditional options include rice, pasta, gnocchi and polenta. Cicheti, which range from basic bar snacks to specialist small plates, tend to get served from lunch time to early evening, using a whole range of fresh food from meatballs to shrimp, baby artichoke, asparagus to more gourmet fantasies. Venice is also a specialist for those with a sweet tooth. These include bussola and zaeti biscuits, pinza (a poor man's cake of humble origins), and the world famous tiramisu. There are many bakeries and cafés offering such a selection; if you are here for a week, you may put on a stone or two. Lastly there is the famous Italian gelato.

Smart restaurants on the Grand Canal

Choices. There are many types of place to eat, from the very expensive Ristorante Danieli with a terrace overlooking the Lagoon over San Giorgio and the Salute, to many places which are far more affordable and traditionally Venetian. Alternatives include:

- A lively square eating outside, maybe overlooking a canal. Many small squares come to life at night and many people miss out one of the best dinning experiences in Venice.

- Back streets, particularly around San Polo, Dorsoduro or Santa Croce. Many restaurants are very small and intimate, and some can be very up market.

- A view of the Lagoon on the Zattere.

- Canal side eating in the Cannaregio.

- There are plenty of options for vegetarians and vegans. Try Frary's opposite the Frari church.

- Along the banks of the Grand Canal at the Rialto.

A nice place for lunch – Campo Aspostoli

Restaurants tend to open from 12.30pm to 2.30pm for lunch and from 6pm to late for dinner, with most restaurants shutting one day a week, and some for longer periods out of season, so do check. Most locals eat around 8pm.

Canal side café – Church of Miracoli

Recommendations. As discussed above, there are so many websites with so many recommendations which are contradictory, you will become even more confused. Going to the no.1 on TripAdvisor many not be the best idea as everyone in trying to book there and you will have very high expectations with a high probability of it not being achieved. Much better to go somewhere else which is different and turns out to be much better than you expected. A happy evening makes a contented traveller and an experience to talk about back home when you have gone somewhere where no one else has been before.

Cafés. They are everywhere. The traditional place to find them is in the squares. Others are in streets which run alongside canals. You can sit inside, but it is much better outside. They provide everything from pastries for breakfast to sandwiches and hot and cold pizza. A much cheaper option than a restaurant for lunch.

Gelato. Italian ice cream is some of the best in the world and there are plenty of gelatos in Venice to try it. Just be aware that prices and portions can vary enormously depending on where you are.

Remote canal side cafes - Dorsoduro

Just go a street or two away from the main tourist areas and thoroughfares where they have to try harder and charge less.

Location. The Dorsoduro, Cannaregio and Castello have the best restaurants and choice, but the other areas are also good, I quite like some of the back street restaurants in San Polo and Santa Croce. The list of areas below describes where different types of restaurants are concentrated:

Via Giuseppe Garibaldi

- San Marco. More expensive because of where it is with high-end traditional restaurants. You will also find concentrations around Campo Stefano, Campo Manin and Campo Luca, and along Calle de la Mandola, Calle Frezzeria, Calle dei Fabbri and Salizada San Lio.

- Dorsoduro. It's all about bistros and bars, many where eating can be reasonably cheap. As well as the Zattere and Campo Margherita, also look down Calle Lunga San Barnaba, Calle della Toletta and Calle Crosera.

- San Polo and Santa Croce. Small lovely little restaurants, mostly buried in the back streets, using fresh produce from the Rialto Markets. Some with canal side views, some high end and some the cheaper pizza trattoria type. Just find one which suits your budget. There is also the strip along the Grand Canal with canal side tables on the Riva dei Vin. Other streets to look at are Fondamenta dei Tolentini, around Campo Giacomo dell'Orio and the back streets around the Rialto Markets.

Mix with the locals

- Cannaregio. Much quieter with traditional cicheti and authentic trattorias with canal side dining. The best places are along Fondamenta Savorgnan, Fondamenta della Sensa and Fondamenta Misericordia. Avoid the places on the main drag through the Lista di Spagna and the Strada Nuovo, where you will find all the junk food tourists can eat, including many well-known burger chains.

- Castello. More remote than the other areas, typically traditional local fare at better prices. The best places are around Campo Giovanni e Paolo, Campo Bandiera e Moro and Via Giuseppe Garibaldi, the latter running up from the Lagoon at the far east end of the city.

Places come alive at night

- Giudecca. Waterfront dining along the Fondamenta delle Zitelle with fantastic views of Venice.

Price and quality. Yes, Venice can be expensive, but contrary to popular perception, it doesn't have to be. You can also eat relatively cheaply. You will find the very best top Michelin-starred or world-class restaurants around San Marco, at a price, but you do not have to sacrifice quality for price. Here are a few tips which may help:

- A simple mediocre sandwich in St Mark's Square can cost the same as a full lunch elsewhere.

Too good to refuse?

- The further you go from St Mark's Square, the cheaper it gets.

- The restaurants with the most ambiance or not in San Marco.

- If going by recommendations, look at a number of websites. Many restaurants lower down TripAdvisor are just as good, but they do not get the volume of tourist reviews to push up their ratings.

- Avoid the congealed pizza bars and sandwich cafés on the main drags from Piazzale Roma or the station to St Mark's.

Queue for gelato

- You do not have to have the full works: a couple of courses, pasta with a starter or dessert will very often fill you up and be sufficient, especially with a litre of house wine or two.

- Look for the fixed menu rather than à la carte.

- Always go into a restaurant that has people already in it, that is lively with atmosphere.

- Sitting by the Grand Canal will command a premium. Quality and service may not be that good as they will always be full and don't have to try.

- Local restaurants are about the same price as in other European cities. Around €30 per head is what you should expect. You can find less. You can double that around St Mark's, and in the best restaurants you can put an extra zero or two on the end.

- Local house wine by the carafe is very good and often half the price or less than a bottle from the wine list. There are also local wines.

- If the menu and a place looks good, try it. It's all about experiencing something new.

Alfresco dinning with a view – Giudecca

To book or not to book? There is no simple answer. The most popular places seem to get booked out early, as will anywhere in the upper echelons of TripAdvisor. That's the way sheep think. The downside to booking in advance is that when you are walking around, you are likely to find somewhere else you like much better. So here are some suggestions:

- Book if you want to go to a particular place.

- If you are walking round and like a place, go in and book for that evening or a couple of nights ahead.

- Book at busy times and in peak seasons.

- Go earlier or later; most restaurants are booked around the 7.30pm standard time.

- It is more exciting to come across a restaurant and decide on the spur of the moment when you get there - and try something different.

Lots of sweet things!

Tipping. When you pay by credit card, don't include a tip, tip the waiter separately in cash. 10% is around the right amount, but how much and how good the service has been is at your discretion.

Picnicking, snacks & drinking water. Officially in Venice, it's illegal to loiter in the street or in public parks while eating, but you're unlikely to be told to move on as long as you observe three cardinal rules:

- Don't picnic or sit in the Piazza San Marco, you will get trampled on anyway.
- Don't picnic or sit on bridges and church steps or upset the Pope.
- Don't drag out a picnic blanket and hamper, the pigeons will tell their mates.

But do buy a sandwich. Venice has many snack bars, pizza-by-the-slice vendors, and Turkish kebab shops where you can eat quickly without paying restaurant prices. Many bakeries sell sandwiches and other prepared foods. You can also find alternatives in the supermarket in Piazzale Roma as well as a few other smaller ones dotted around the city. I quite like getting a hot sandwich and sitting out on the Grand Canal near the Rialto and watching the boats go by.

Don't waste money on bottled water in Venice. The public tap water is safe, cold and tastes great. It's piped in from deep wells on the Italian mainland, and it's so good that it has its own brand name, Acqua Veritas. Nearly every square has a fountain where you can fill your water bottle.

TOP TIP: A good evening out is not about how much you spend. A relaxed happy restaurant with good food and good ambiance is a great experience to remember. It will also be more impressive to the important lady than the size of the bill.

TOP TIP: If you are in the gelateria queue and the person in front only gets a small dollop of ice cream, go somewhere else. Avoid gelatos in the main tourist drag and squares. You get less and pay more.

An Aperol helps the medicine go down

Shopping and spending your money on nice things

There are a lot of interesting and delightful things to buy in Venice from top range Italian goods down to the best gold-plated souvenirs and tourist trash money can buy. How much you pay for it depends on where you buy it and how discerning you are. Venice is full of rip-offs, but you can also buy some good stuff, including Italian clothes, accessories, art and Murano glass. You just have to look carefully at what you buy and how much you really think it's worth. Prices for the same item can vary wildly, so shop around. If you are looking for traditional Venetian products, be wary because much of the cheaper stuff is imported in from other areas of Italy or the Far East and is not Venetian at all.

Glass ornaments

For visitors from outside the European Union, you may able to reclaim the VAT tax at customs when you leave Italy. Retain your receipts.

The most exclusive shops are to be found in the streets surrounding St Mark's Square, where high-limit credit cards and gullible tourists abound. For original fashion and better value, venture into the back streets, away from the global brands. Many shops will ship worldwide. Here is some insight into what to buy:

- Art, sculpture and glass. Many artists who produce originals work in Venice. Look for the back street studios, where you can see the work being produced. For Murano glass, look for the Murano trademarks and certificate of authentication.

Best Italian gloves

- Clothing. Italian style and design is a world leader, with clothing made from top quality fabrics. Here you can find unique hand-printed dresses or top quality items which will be different from the global brands.

- Accessories. Quality leather shoes and handbags are everywhere. You will find individual items that cannot be mass produced, so you can stand out and look the part in a crowd. Glass-blown necklaces, delightful hand-beaten copper and silver bracelets and custom-fit shoes. And traditional Venetian masks. There is plenty to choose from.

- Jewellery. Imaginative modern jewellery mixing glass with precious stones.

- Home decor. Luxury homemade textiles from top Italian designers. Modern homeware, elegant objects, ceramics and lamps of individual choice.

- Eyewear. Stylish frames and sunglasses. Just bring your subscription and get your own special pair.

Little corner shops and stands

127

- Antiques. A hub of treasures and period pieces of a bygone age, including paintings, furniture, lamps and glassware, many of which have their origin in the past from the many palazzos of Venice.

- Glass. Of course, Murano glass, some of the best artistic glass in the world. Look for glass trinkets too.

And where do you find all this stuff? When out on your wanderings through the city, keep your eyes open, as you will find many interesting places. Many are tucked away. The main shopping streets are the alleys along the Mercerie, which runs between St Mark's and the Rialto. You'll find exclusive shopping between St Mark's and the Accademia Bridge, and more reasonable and interesting shops between the Rialto and Campo San Polo. Each area tends to have a characteristic of its own. Here is where to look:

Some shops are scarier than others

- San Marco. Art galleries, high-end international designers and global brands and galleries.

- Dorsoduro. Antique shops and fashion boutiques.

- San Polo and Santa Croce. Artists' back street studios, glass, paper and fashion.

- Cannaregio and Murano. High street bargains along the main drag, and art bargains. On the islands, lace and world-renowned glass.

- Castello. Newer artisans and individual curios shops.

- Giudecca and Southern Islands. Heritage textiles, paper-made design and sculptural knits.

A fine masterpiece Italian of machinery

Arts and museums

Art and museums everywhere

Because of its history and heritage and now as a world leading tourist destination, Venice is full of art galleries and museums. If you want to see Venice from an original perspective, you need to see the art and architecture in its original settings such as churches and palazzos. Depending on your depth of interest, there are so many places to see. The perception of what is interesting and how long to spend is personal, everyone is different. But if it is your mission, my suggestion is to get a detailed guide book and list all the places and locations you want to see before you go, as many are very close to one another. Here are some of the key ones you could consider:

- Churches: Frari, Basilica (St Mark's), Giovanni e Paolo, Santa Maria dei Miracoli, and San Salvador, for key art works and architecture.

- Palazzos: Ducale (Doge's), Mocenigo, Ca' Rezzonico and Ca' d'Oro.

- Museums: Museo Civico Correr and Ca' Pesaro.
- Galleries: Accademia, Scuola Grande di San Rocco and Peggy Guggenheim Collection.

Bars, night life and entertainment

Although Venice may not be one of the drunken party capitals of the world, it has plenty of bars, night life and entertainment, especially during the festivals.

St Marco is expensive – local is much cheaper

Bars. Bars vary from the cheap to the very exclusive. A couple of Bellinis in Harry's Bar may set you back more than a night's drinking in Campo Margherita. Likewise, a round of drinks sitting at the tables watching the orchestras at one of the bars in St Mark's Square will do serious damage to your credit card. Bars vary from exclusive cocktail bars around San Marco to wine bars, pubs and clubs. Venice has a fine choice of wines. Top drinks are Spritz, local wines, Prosecco and Morgana beer.

Many cafés turn into bars at night time. There is a happy hour, or two, which starts around 6pm, and is quite a social affair, mixed with a few cicheti or bar snacks. Having

Harry's Bar

drinks sitting down and being served can cost twice as much as standing up by the bar. Pubs and wine bars tend to stay open to between 1am to 2am. Prices vary widely from local bars where drinks are €2 to €3, to San Marco, where you can pay €16 upwards.

Bars vary enormously, from high-end cocktail and wine bars around San Marco to the small local bars with live music in San Polo, Santa Croce and the Dorsoduro. Or you can watch the world go by on the Zattere with fabulous views of the Lagoon. A newer addition is the Skyline bar at the top of the Hilton Molino Stucky at the end of the Giudecca, where you

can drink and dip in the pool at the same time. This used to be an old derelict flour mill - how times do change. There are also a number of clubs where you can drink to the small hours of the morning including the Martini Scala Club piano bar in San Marco and Piccolo Mondo in the Dorsoduro. The bars in Castello and Cannaregio tend to be more local, but many are very enjoyable with canal side drinking.

Drinking tends to be considerate, as sound travels and Venice quietens down after about 10pm. For any rowdies, the locals have a habit

Thirsty work this messing about in boats

of pouring water out of upstairs windows; better than the medieval days, when the dousing was with boiling oil.

Music. Venice caters for all tastes from classical and opera, to rock and pop. La Fenice is one of Europe's top opera houses. Venice is also a good place to hear classical music in its original setting as previous generations did. Many of the palazzos and churches hold concerts. There is nothing like experiencing a classical concert in the acoustics of one of the big churches. It is best to look at the websites to see what is on. Try www.interpretiveneziani.com, www.venezia.unica.it or the individual web sites for the theatres. You can also find jazz and rock and pop; try Bacaro Jazz in San Marco, Venice Jazz Club near Campo Santa Margherita, or other bars with live music.

La Fenice

Bacaro Jazz near the Rialto Bridge

Theatre and Film. As well as the La Fenice, Venice has a number of other theatres including Teatro Malibran and Teatro Goldoni, one of the oldest theatres in the city, which has an excellent programme of international plays performed in Italian. Or try Teatro Fondamenta Nuovo which hosts contemporary dance, experimental jazz music and films. The Auditorium Santa Margherita sometimes stages musical performances for free. Cinemas can be found at Giorgione Movie d'Essai in Cannaregio and Multisala Astra in the Lido. In the summer there are outdoor concerts and cinemas set up in some of the squares, particularly Campo San Polo. Also remember that Venice has featured as the backdrop in many famous films, including *Casino Royale*, *Death in Venice* and *The Wings of the Dove*. See if you can spot the locations.

There are many packages which combine dinner at a nice restaurant with a concert or a show; see www.veneziaunica.it, but compare prices as they can differ quite a lot for the same programme.

Festivals

Venice is full of festivals, expos and events most the year round except December and January. It is best to check what's on for a list of current events. Also book early for the key ones, including accommodation if you want some. Festivals range from the Carnevale to art, film and fashion events. Here are some of the key ones:

It's all about contentment

- Carnevale. A two-week street party in February of costumes and masked balls. www.carnevale.venezia.it.

- Venice International Film Festival. Late August to early September. Movie stars bowel up to make the most of the weather, and red carpets and regattas play a big part. www.labiennale.org.

- Regata Storica. Again, in September, a 16th-century pageant of costumes and eight oared gondolas including parades and races, provide dramatic action to the backdrop of the Grand Canal. www.regatastoricavenezia.it

- Biennale di Venezia. Running between May and November, Europe's premier art showcase, with contemporary art and architecture on alternate years. www.labiennale.org

- Venice Jazz Festival. In July, international legends play in all sorts of venues, including the La Fenice and the Peggy Guggenheim Collection in the Dorsoduro. www.venetojazz.com

Venice is full of artists

- Venezia Suona. On a Sunday in June or July, bands play live music in many of the squares and streets throughout the city with a grand concert in St Mark's Square. Check out www.veneziasuona.it.

Ponte dei Tri Achi

131

Different worlds intersecting

Best washing – Campo Santa Marina

And the band plays on... – St Mark's Square

Chapter 11 - A Bit of History, But Not Too Much

The early days and the Romans

Did you know that Venice was founded on a malarial infested swamp circa 1500 BC? A place full of mossies, hot and humid in the summer time, which was not a nice place to live. The Veneti were the first known native people to have settled along the northern Adriatic coast from around 800 BC.

Venice was built on many islands

Long before Venice emerged from the Lagoon, the Romans are thought to have built a town called Altinum, which has been discovered near Marco Polo Airport, without the runways and aeroplanes. The Romans were masters of building in the swampy environment and, from the archaeology discovered to date, were thought to have built on the islands in the network of canals and rivers which lead into the Lagoon. Many of the local Veneti then fled to the islands in the Lagoon.

The gondola was invented, but not so good in the rain

The Romans lasted from around 49 AD to the 5th/6th centuries AD, being driven out by the Visigoths, Huns and Lombards and other unsavoury barbaric regimes from the north. Altinum played a major role in Venice's history as one of the richest Roman settlements, but inhabitants fled before the advance of the armies of Attila the Hun. Then as water levels rose, the abandoned city sank into the Lagoon, so it is not the first time Venice has had this problem. Its walls remain covered by fields today. And this is why the ancient city has remained undiscovered for such a long time.

Mediterranean trade and the Doges

Venice used to be at the centre of Mediterranean maritime trade, from Syria and Constantinople in the East to Spain in the West. Salt, spice and other goodies arrived through the Silk Route. As the displaced Veneti communities grew, Venice rose from the Lagoon and was established around 460 AD. In 726 AD, Orso Ipato was elected leader and was made the first Doge. The Doges were set to lead the city for the next 1000 years. But being a Doge was not good for long lasting mortality; most

Picture perfect – the Grand Canal from the Salute

of the early Doges did not last long and died an unnatural death, either being assassinated or deposed for overstepping their authority.

Venice grew and thrived. The earth was drained and the city was built on wooden piles,

mainly larch, driven into the soft silt to sit above the tides of the Lagoon. Rather than rotting, the wooden piles underwent a vitrification process as the surrounding sediments kept the oxygen out. From the 900s AD, the city's business interests expanded; Venice was the intermediary between the Western Roman and Byzantine empires and established lucrative contracts equipping the Holy Land Crusaders. But with rivals in Pisa and Genoa, all was not so straight forward, so Venice established its superiority and power by putting together a formidable navy. Shipyards and production lines were created in the Arsenale capable of turning out a warship a day, which was something quite considerable in those days, not like now with the UK producing one new aircraft carrier every 20 years.

Murano glass was created

Architecture and St Mark's

Venice has a whole range of architectures: Byzantine, Romanesque, Renaissance palaces, Neoclassical, Gothic cathedrals and Baroque. This has resulted in creation of many fantastic buildings, including beautiful marble clad churches and palaces. Fortunately, the city has not added many of the more modern and hideous examples, like brutalist 1960s concrete blocks or 1990s Dubaiesque glass towers. Most of that has been confined to the mainland.

Houses were built on wooden piles

St Mark's Square was created from a bag of bones

The story of St Mark starts in 828 AD, when smugglers stole the holy bones of St Mark the Evangelist from Alexandria and brought them back to Venice disguised as a load of old pork. According to legend, St Mark had visited the Lagoon and been told that his body would rest there. So, his body was buried in the Basilica of St Mark's (San Marco) and he became the patron saint of Venice and the square was named after him.

134

Venice in 1612 – can you tell what has changed?

The dodgy Doges were hard bargaining and smart dealers who helped the city thrive and new industries of glass blowing, jewellery, embroidered lace making and paper making were established. The Doges used their leverage and position to load their ships with the booty, including smelly sausages, from faraway lands they had pillaged, just like some of the big corporates do today. They were always having spats with their local rivals. One day Genoa tried to invade Venice, but failed because they made a strategic error. They tried to starve the city out instead of invading, but Venice outsmarted them having already prepared for such an event and, in the interim, they built many ships, shored up the defences and sent the Genoese packing.

Death by plague and Venice's decline

But it was not all good for normal Venetians. The ruling elite wielded an iron fist. A shadowy secret police force, the Consiglio dei Diece, thwarted conspiracies by deploying secret agents throughout

Many bridges and canals

the city to spy on its own people, and those in many European capitals. People used to disappear and trials, torture and executions took place in secret. But compared with its barbaric neighbours, Venice was still a relatively tolerant place.

A cemetery was built nearby for lots of dead

But Venice also had its bad times. In 1348 the Black Plague arrived, originating from rats unloaded in the Dorsoduro docks. Quarantine stations were created to halt the spread of the bubonic plague, Venice being the first city in Europe to adopt such a process with success. But the plague did kill 60% of the population which makes today's cases of Chinese bird flu look pretty tame.

In 1492, Christopher Columbus started off a new stage of world discovery, and Venice's slow road into obsolescence began, with Portugal and Spain taking over as the top dogs, trading with the Americas and cutting out Venice's customs controls and trade altogether. But other industries grew. In 1494, the first portable-size books were printed in Venice by the printer Aldus Manutius, presaging the trend centuries later where paperback books are available in every high street, railway station and airport departures lounge. By 1500, one in six books published in Europe was printed in Venice.

The original hospital still exists today

Interesting architecture

In 1516 there was a proclamation that all Jews should live in a separated area called the Ghetto, with the gates locked and guarded after dark. The Ghetto still exists today, without the gates and the guards, but many Jews still live there. This is a wonderful area to visit and features in one of the walks in this book, in Chapter 8.

Decadence and opulence

The 1600s was the start of the age of decadence and scandals; Venice was the centre of the cosmopolitan social scene with parties, music, opera, fancy clothes, women and art - although not all at the same time. But it did include monstrous hair dos and hideously high 50cm platform shoes. The theatres and much of the famous art was created during this period, and many opulent palaces were built. The palaces were known as palazzos and the main entrance was usually from the water, entering into a large hall.

By the end of the 16th century, through various laws and to distinguish themselves, there were over 12,000 ladies of the night riding around in gondolas with red lights. It was also a bad period. The city had two very bad plagues, one in 1575 and another in 1630; over a third of the population died in the latter. As well as hospitals created for the plague victims, there were numerous hospices built for the many courtesans who caught other nasty diseases.

Masks and extravagant hair dos

Venetian masks are a centuries-old tradition of Venice. The masks are typically worn during the Carnival, but have been used on many other occasions in the past, usually as a device for hiding the wearer's identity and social status. You will find many different masks in the shops which you can buy and wear to work today.

As the old painters saw it – not much seems to have changed since

More battles and occupation

Venice was also still having spats with the church, and succeeded in reducing the revenue to Rome by closing churches. However, it was less successful in its battle with the Ottomans, to whom it lost Crete. On the spat with the Roman Catholic Church, Venice conducted an audit of the revenues paid to Rome in the previous decade of 11 million golden ducats, a huge sum in those days. In its battle with the Ottomans, a deal was struck enabling Venice to retain prime coastal territory and nominal control.

In the 16th and 17th centuries, Venice lost out further as Portuguese trade to the Far East was routed round Africa, as the Suez Canal had not been built yet, but was being thought about. Then Napoleon turned up in 1797 and occupied the place, grabbing any art which was not nailed down. He was only around for 15 years, before being pushed out by the Austrians in 1814, who imposed heavy taxes which pushed the Venice to starvation and destitution, a complete transformation from the riches it once had.

Some of the new occupiers were not very nice people

Many famous people have lived or were born in Venice, including Antonio Vivaldi, **Giacomo Casanova**, Titian, Marco Polo and Pope Paul II. There are many more, so I apologise for all those I have missed and if your name is not on the list.

The later years

In 1836 the first opera house burnt down. A new one was built, which also burnt down, in 1996 and was rebuilt in 2003. In 1846, the first train arrived in Venice over the new Causeway, so Venice was no longer cut off from the mainland. Then in 1866, Venice became part of Italy of which it remains today.

During the 19th century, glamorous Venice took on a more mundane industrial role, with factories springing up along the Giudecca and textile industries in Mestre and the surrounding area on the mainland. During the First World War, the incompetent Austro-Hungarian planes dropped almost 300 bombs on Venice, but most missed. After the war, in 1933, Mussolini built the Freedom Bridge beside the railway along the Causeway, the only car access to Venice. During the Second World War, a large number of Jews were rounded up and taken away. The city itself was lucky and came out of the war unscathed.

The Causeway was built

Many new arrivals!

Over the centuries, a number of ghosts have been spotted. In Campo St Barnaba, a French crusader died a dishonourable death before getting to the Holy Land. Also, Fosca Loredan is said to emerge from the Grand Canal, not far from the Rialto Bridge with the head of his wife, Elena, which he cut off in a rage of jealousy. So when you go down the dimly lit back alleys on a dark foggy night, there is a good chance you may bump into one of them.

In 1966, the old reminder about a sinking Venice came as a wake-up call, with disastrous floods which reached two metres higher than sea level. Something had to be done, but it would take a long time. In 1973 the first law was passed to put a barrier across the Lagoon with completion in 1995. In 2018, it has still not been completed; arguments, corruption and scientific evidence of the fragile nature of the Lagoon continue to undermine the idea. Because of the floods and the inconvenience of working in Venice, much of the population has now left. Only 55,000 Venetians remain.

More recently in 2018, there has been a plan to revamp St Mark's Square for the first time in over 500 years. A new conference and exhibition facility will be created in the restoration of the Procuratie Vecchie on the north side, creating much needed new jobs. Also the dilapidated gardens on the south side between the Square and the Lagoon are going to receive attention.

To the future?

Since then the problems of Venice have got worse, not just with the tide of water, but with the tide of people. Cruise ships and cheap travel have enabled even more people to visit

But some things cannot change

the city. In addition, speedboats are eroding the foundations and increasing pollution in the Lagoon. There is talk of restricting the number of visitors, but as the city now relies on tourist revenue for the jobs, the authorities are in a quandary. The 100,000 cruise ship passengers in 1999 have grown to over 3 million in 2014 with an additional 60,000 visitors a day who come by other means. With only nine public toilets and only one on Murano, I am not sure where they are all going to go.

San Giorgio Maggiore from the Campanile

Rio de San Barnaba – Dorsoduro

Chapter 12 - Other Useful Stuff

Venice is one of Europe's major tourist cities and generally has all the facilities one would expect. But because of its age, architecture, and large number of people who visit in a small space, it has its challenges. But go with it, as it is a pity to let these little things ruin a visit to such a beautiful place. The check list below should help make the domestic things a little bit easier.

Just adds to the ambience

- Climate and what to wear. Spring is damp and summer is crowded and hot, 28°C. Autumn offers warm days at 15°C, with lower hotel rates, while winter is chilly. Although the days can be nice in spring and autumn, it can be very chilly when the sun goes down. Venice is also prone to sudden rain storms even in the summer, so be prepared when out and about.
- Churches. Bare shoulders and shorts are frowned upon. Also, many do not allow photography and the Basilica in St Mark's does not allow cameras in at all.
- Disabled travellers. 70% of Venice and the vaporetto are accessible by wheelchair. But there are many bridges and steps which are difficult and will slow you down, so careful planning of your route is required. A Venezia Accessible information pack is available online or from the tourist office.
- Electricity. 220v AC with two-pin European plugs or adaptors.

View of the Grand Canal from the new Costituzione Bridge

141

- Etiquette. Try and speak a bit of Italian, it is appreciated and very often rewarded with better service. Smoking is allowed in bars but not on the vaporetto.
- Gay and lesbian. Legal in Italy and generally accepted in Venice.
- Health. For emergencies, go to the SS Giovanni e Paolo Hospital in Castello. Dial 118 for an ambulance. The standard of healthcare in Venice is generally good. Pharmacies are open from 8.30am to 12.30pm and 3.30pm to 7.30pm.

Scuola Grande di San Marco

Hotel Gabrielli, upmarket hotel

- Internet access. Available in most hotels although some rooms with thick walls may have difficulty. Available in some cafés, but connection can also be purchased from Venezia Unica from €5 for 24 hours.
- Language. Mostly Italian, but many menus in English and some in French.
- Money. Italy uses the euro (€). Most places except cafés tend to take credit or debit cards. Banks tend to open from 8.30am to 1.30pm Monday to Friday, but there are plenty of accessible 24hr ATMs.

The lighthouse on Murano and the island of San Michele from the Misericordia marina

- Personal security. Venice is a safe city, even for single women at night, and is one of the safest places for women travellers, but the usual sensible precautions should still be applied. Just watch for pickpockets around Piazzale Roma and the station.
- Police. In an emergency, dial 112.
- Time Zone. Venice is 1 hour ahead of GMT.
- Tipping. Most Italians just leave small change, €0.20 or so, but 10% in restaurants.
- Toilets. A public toilet is a rare sight, there are only 9 scattered around Venice to satisfy the needs of all those millions of visitors, at €1.50 a time. They are suitable for people with disabilities. Look for the WC signs, they are not always easy to find. Cafés and restaurants reserve their toilets for paying customers, another excuse to have a coffee. Beware, many toilets do not have seats and can be tricky to use.

Restaurant with a view, Giudecca

TOP TIP: Always take the opportunity to go when you have a chance.

- Tourist information. The main offices are at the airport, Piazzale Roma, St Mark's Square and at the station. Some useful websites:
  - o Venice City Tourist and Travel, www.veneziaunica.it
  - o Government Tourist Board, www.italia.it/en/discover-italy/veneto.html
  - o Turismo Venezia, www.turismovenezia.it
- Visas and passports. Venice is in Italy, which is part of the European Union (EU). You should ensure that you have a valid passport and any necessary visas to enter the EU.

St Mark's panorama in the evening light from the Lagoon vaporetto

Campo Mori – local square in the Cannaregio

Index

Index

Index

Farewell from the Campanile of St Marks – Hope you have a good trip

Lightning Source UK Ltd.
Milton Keynes UK
UKHW02f0713111018

330372UK00009B/76/P